TOP **10**
MONTENEGRO

W0113951

CONTENTS

MONTENEGRO

INTRODUCING

Budva Old Town

WELCOME TO
MONTENEGRO

A trip to Montenegro is one for the books. With its stunning beaches, epic mountains and picture-perfect coastal towns, this Balkan beauty never fails to enchant. With Top 10 Montenegro, you'll enjoy the very best the country has to offer.

Making waves on the Adriatic coast, Montenegro has cemented itself on tourist itineraries – and it's about time. Few countries have such an abundance of natural beauty in such a compact space. On the coast, sandy beaches and shimmering coves tempt beachgoers, and more than rival Montenegro's Adriatic neighbour, Croatia. Inland, vast lakes teem with birdlife and huge caves gape under the ground. Yet it's in the country's north that the most thrilling landscapes await. Here, in the wilds of Montenegro, peaks rise like untamed giants, verdant valleys

Autumn scenery in Montenegro

pool with glacial lakes and shady forests shelter a wealth of wildlife (including elusive brown bears and Balkan lynx). It's hardly surprising that this is prime hiking territory, but there's plenty of other activities on offer, too: think whitewater rafting, zip-lining, cycling and paragliding.

While it has spectacular scenery in spades, Montenegro is more than just a pretty face. In the country's centre, the capital of Podgorica packs a punch with its top-notch bars, restaurants and art galleries. Meanwhile, the old royal centre of Cetinje offers a clutch of charming museums and grand monuments. Then there's the towns along the coast. In the Bay of

Kotor, postcard-worthy places like Perast, Herceg Novi and Kotor promise Venetian-era architecture, beautiful churches and epic views of the surrounding mountains. Further down, party-loving Budva entices young travellers while Ulcinj offers history in abundance (plus it's within spitting distance of the country's most popular beaches).

So, where to start? With Top 10 Montenegro, of course. This pocket-sized guide gets to the heart of the country with simple lists of 10, expert local knowledge and comprehensive maps, helping you turn an ordinary trip into an extraordinary one.

THE STORY OF
MONTENEGRO

Montenegro's history is fiendishly complex. Ruled over by a succession of invaders and occupiers, before being enmeshed in a fractious Yugoslav federation, the country finally gained full independence in 2006. Here's the story of how it came to be.

Early Settlement

Archaeological remains suggest that the area of present-day Montenegro was settled in the Palaeolithic and Neolithic eras. Yet things didn't really kick off until around 5 BCE when an Indigenous Illyrian kingdom – a loose confederation of Indo-European people in the eastern Adriatic – emerged here. Around the same time, the Greeks began to establish trading centres along the country's coast. Clocking the potential for trade, the Romans soon swooped in, defeating the Illyrians and founding the province of Dalmatia – which incorporated most of Montenegro and Croatia – in 297 CE. As Roman power waned in the fifth century, this area witnessed repeated incursions by semi-nomadic invaders such as the Goths and the Huns.

The Slavs' New State

By the middle of the 7th century, these semi-nomadic groups had been supplanted by the Slavs, who comprised three disparate groups: the Slovenes, who settled in northern Dalmatia; the Croats in the west; and the Serbs, who settled in the area of present-day Montenegro. By the end of the 10th century, the Serbs had established the Slav state of Duklja (or Doclea). Later referred to as Zeta, this land was then incorporated into the powerful Serbian state of Raška, headed up by the dominant Nemanjić family. Not satisfied with simply ruling over a huge swathe of land (including Serbia, Kosovo and Montenegro), the Nemanjićs also sought to establish an independent Orthodox Church. This led to the

Romans battling the Illyrians, early inhabitants of Montenegro

Forces from the Ottoman Empire entering Montenegro

founding of numerous monastic churches such as Morača, north of Podgorica, in 1252.

The Prince-Bishops

Despite being the most dominant medieval state in the Balkans, the Serbian Empire eventually fell, but other occupiers were waiting in the wings. In the 14th and 15th centuries, the Republic of Venice began to assert control over the coast, making Kotor its stronghold. The Ottoman Empire was also gaining power in the Balkans around this time, and moved to tighten its grip on inland Montenegro.

Despite the turmoil, this was a time of great cultural progress for Montenegro: a flurry of Orthodox monasteries were constructed and Europe's first printing house was established in Cetinje. Responsibility for both the state and the church was given over to a succession of prince-bishops (bishops who were also civil rulers), none more powerful than the Petrović clan, among whose number was the poet Petar II Petrović-Njegoš.

Acknowledged as an independent principality in 1798, Montenegro didn't gain independence until the Congress of Berlin in 1878, when Cetinje was conferred as the new capital. In 1910, the country was then elevated to the status of a constitutional monarchy. In the process, Prince Nikola – head of the House of Petrović-Njegoš – declared himself king, the country's first and only.

Moments in History

297 CE
After defeating the Illyrians, the Romans establish the province of Dalmatia, which incorporates most of present-day Montenegro.

Late 10th century
Serbs establish the Slav state of Duklja (or Doclea), which roughly encompasses the territories of modern-day southeastern Montenegro.

1276
The name "Crna Gora" (Montenegro) is mentioned for the first time in the Charter of King Milutin. Meaning "Black Mountain", it's likely named after the dense forests that cover Mount Lovćen.

1697
The first of the Petrović-Njegoš house, Danilo I Petrović-Njegoš, comes to power.

1878
Montenegrin independence is recognized at the Congress of Berlin.

1929

After World War I, Montenegro becomes part of the Kingdom of Yugoslavia, a dictatorial monarchy in the Balkans.

1945

Together with Serbia, Slovenia, Macedonia, Croatia and Bosnia, Montenegro becomes part of the new Socialist Federal Republic of Yugoslavia under Josip Broz Tito.

1992

Rising nationalist and independence aspirations bring bloody conflict in neighbouring Bosnia; Montenegro remains part of Yugoslavia.

2006

In a countrywide referendum, just over 55 per cent of the population vote for independence, and in June Montenegro becomes the 192nd member of the United Nations.

2017

Montenegro joins NATO (the North Atlantic Treaty Organization).

The Era of Yugoslavia

After fighting in the Serbian campaign during World War I, Montenegro was subsumed into the dictatorial Kingdom of Yugoslavia in 1929. Just decades after gaining its independence, this was a crushing blow to the nation's renewed sense of self. Another blow came in the 1940s, when Montenegro was occupied first by Italy, and then Nazi Germany, during World War II. Locals, however, fought back, leading an uprising against the occupation. The country was eventually liberated, but remained in the grip of the newly named Socialist Federal Republic of Yugoslavia. Although Montenegro had its own administration, it was ultimately directed and under the full control of the Socialist party, and President Josep Broz Tito.

Rising nationalist and independence aspirations among the constituent republics led to Yugoslavia's eventual implosion in the 1990s, culminating in a succession of bloody wars. One by one, Slovenia, Macedonia, Croatia and Bosnia-Hercegovina broke away from the Yugoslav Federation, leaving just Montenegro and Serbia – who formed the eponymous state of Serbia and Montenegro. In 1991, the leader of the Democratic Party of Socialists (DPS), Milo Djukanović was inaugurated as the Montenegrin prime minister (with the blessing of Serbian President Slobodan Milošević). He became the longest-ruling contemporary politician in Europe.

Montenegrin soldiers in World War I

Supporters celebrating Montenegrin independence in 2006

Towards Independence

Following the ousting of Serbian president Slobodan Milošević by pro-Western reformers in 2000, the Montenegrin leadership became increasingly independence-minded. As a result, in May 2006 the country held its first referendum – just over 55 per cent voted in favour of a split with Serbia. This marked the final demise of the multinational state, and in June that year Montenegro became the last of the original six Yugoslav republics to gain its independence. Yet it wasn't all smooth-sailing. The Balkan wars of the 1990s had left a major scar on the region, with hyperinflation rife and few travellers tempted to venture here (leaving the country reliant on visitors from Serbia and Russia).

Montenegro Today

Today, the picture is very different. Tourism plays a huge role in the country's economy, with visitors from all over drawn to Montenegro's picturesque coastline and wild interior; it's certainly no longer the secret destination it once was. There has also been seismic change in the country's political landscape in recent years, not least in the 2020 general election, which resulted in the fall from power of the once mighty Democratic Party of Socialists, which had ruled the country since the introduction of multi-party politics in 1990, and a victory for the opposition parties – For the Future of Montenegro, Peace is Our Nation and In Black and White. On the international front, Montenegro joined NATO in 2017, but its accession to the European Union – something that many Montenegrins aspire to and which has been on the agenda since 2012 – is still some years off.

Budva's lovely coastline, a major draw for tourists

TOP 10
EXPERIENCES

Planning the perfect trip to Montenegro? Whether you're visiting for the first time or making a return trip, there are some things you simply shouldn't miss out on. To make the most of your time – and to enjoy the very best this beautiful country has to offer – be sure to add these experiences to your list.

1 Visit the Bay of Kotor
More reminiscent of a fjord than a bay, this epic landscape of hulking cliffs, picturesque towns and shimmering waters is Montenegro's calling card *(p82)*. Whether you choose to explore the area by boat or by car, you're guaranteed postcard-worthy views at every turn.

2 Join the festivities
Time your visit to coincide with one of the country's festivals *(p76)* and you'll be in for a treat. Kotor hosts the most extravagant celebrations, with its lively Winter Carnival and sea-themed Boka Nights. Meanwhile in Herceg Novi, the blooming of mimosas is met with stunning masquerade balls.

3 Bask on the beach
Montenegro's beautiful coastline more than rivals that of its Adriatic neighbours. With sweeping sandy beaches, clandestine coves and pebbly pockets, the western shoreline is primed for swimming and sunbathing. The country is also famed for its windsurfing – Velika Plaža *(p100)* is a go-to.

4 Try Njeguši prosciutto
The country's most lauded culinary treat *(p72)*, Njeguši prosciutto hails from the small mountain village of the same name. It's famous for good reason: undergoing a meticulous process of salting, seasoning and air-drying, the ham takes months to prepare and is prized across the country.

5 Explore historic towns

Hosting treasures from the Venetian and Ottoman empires, Montenegro's old towns are open-air history museums. But they're also vibrant holiday hot spots, with buzzy bars and traditional restaurants hidden down atmospheric alleyways.

6 Raft the Tara River

There's no better way to explore Europe's deepest canyon (p113) than by rafting through it. Routes along the Tara River afford spectacular views (the towering Đurđevića Tara Bridge is a highlight), with numerous rapids providing thrills and spills aplenty.

7 Spot Dalmatian pelicans

Bird-watchers will have a field day in Montenegro. From soaring golden eagles to nimble alpine swifts, this country is a haven for birdlife, and none are more special than the Dalmatian pelicans, most commonly seen around Lake Skadar (p26).

8 Conquer the peaks

Sure Montenegro is famed for its beaches, but its mountains are equally epic. These craggy karst giants loom in the country's north, promising out-of-this-world hikes and a host of outdoor activities. Head to Durmitor National Park (p22) for the best of them.

9 Go to church

With so many beautiful religious monuments, it's a battle for the country's most famous. Carved into a cliff face, Ostrog Monastery (p48) is an amazing site, but Our Lady of the Rocks (p84), on an island in the Bay of Kotor, is perhaps the country's most iconic.

10 Take a road trip

Travelling by car is arguably the best way to explore this compact country, and you only need a few hours to move between its varied landscapes. One moment you'll be racing along the coast, the next you'll be tackling scenic switchbacks in the mountains.

ITINERARIES

Exploring the Bay of Kotor, hiking through Durmitor's snowy peaks, museum-hopping in Cetinje: there's a lot to see and do in Montenegro. With places to eat, drink or take in the view, these itineraries offer ways to spend 2 and 7 days in the country.

2 DAYS IN KOTOR

Day 1

Morning
Rise early and fuel up with a hearty breakfast: the first thing on your Kotor itinerary is a hike. The historic town's old fortress walls *(p69)* wind their way up the cliffside, offering epic views of the town and the surrounding Bay of Kotor. It's a short and steep climb that takes around 90 minutes there and back. After soaking up the superlative views, head down to Trg od Drva (Wood Square) for a cooling beverage on the flower-scented terrace of Bastion *(restoranbastion.com)*. You'll see dozens of street cats lazing in the sun outside, but more of them tomorrow. From here, wander down to Trg Sv Luke (St Luke's Square), home to the eponymous church – a tiny, but fascinating structure – before lunching on grilled octopus at Pržun *(przun.me)*.

Buzzy Trg Sv Luke, and its historic church

> 🧋 **DRINK**
> A short walk from Kotor's cathedral is Nitrox *(p90)*, a dinky bar serving a selection of craft beers. While it gets particularly lively at night, its outdoor seating area is lovely and chilled in the afternoon, perfect for a pint.

Afternoon
Batteries recharged, it's time to delve into the region's illustrious history. Start at the superb Maritime Museum *(p52)*, housed within an elegant palatial building; the model ships are particularly delightful. From here, pass through a couple more picturesque squares to St Tryphon's Cathedral *(p54)*. Kotor's most important ecclesiastical building sports a magnificent rib-vaulted ceiling and Gothic windows. Spend the rest of your afternoon ambling around the Old Town, soaking up the atmosphere and popping into a bar or two. As evening approaches, make your way towards the water for dinner at Galion *(p91)* – the fabulous seafood repertoire here features local dishes such as squid-ink risotto.

Day 2

Morning
You can't visit the Bay of Kotor without taking to the water, so on your second day, make for the harbour. From here

VIEW
While Kotor's old fortress walls provide a popular viewpoint of the bay, the belfry of Perast's Church of St Nicholas is almost as good. Note that the staircase is quite steep and the ceiling low.

you can take a 60-minute, high-octane speedboat trip up the coast to Perast. The bay's most irresistible spot, this picture-perfect waterfront town is lined with stately palaces and pristine townhouses. After wandering around, hop on a water-taxi bound for the islet of Our Lady of the Rock *(p84)*, one of the country's most photographed spots. Back on the mainland, indulge in lunch by the water at the Hotel Conte's *(p128)* fabulous restaurant before returning to Kotor.

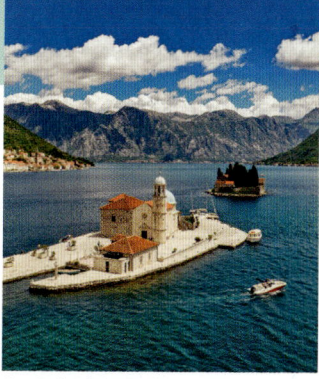

Our Lady of the Rocks, an island off the coast of Perast

Afternoon

Come afternoon, peruse the buzzy market stalls lining the entrance of Kotor's Old Town, then make your way through the pink-tinged Sea Gate *(p32)* into Trg od Oružja (Arms Square). This café-strewn space is known for its amusingly askew clock tower – the result of one too many earthquakes. Your last port of call before dinner is the surprisingly entertaining Cat Museum *(p53)*, stuffed with all kinds of cat-themed memorabilia (the small fee goes towards feeding local felines). Finally, it's time to bid farewell to the bay with a delicious Mediterranean dinner at Ladovina Kitchen and Wine Bar *(p91)*.

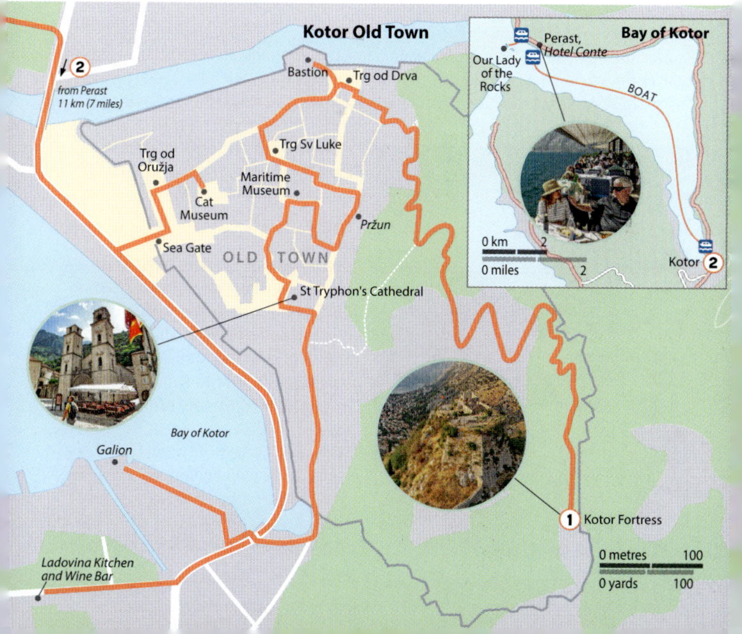
Kotor Old Town
2
from Perast
11 km (7 miles)
Bastion
Trg od Drva
Trg Sv Luke
Trg od Oružja
Maritime Museum
Cat Museum
Pržun
Sea Gate
OLD TOWN
St Tryphon's Cathedral
Bay of Kotor
Galion
Ladovina Kitchen and Wine Bar
1
Kotor Fortress
0 metres 100
0 yards 100
Bay of Kotor
Perast, Hotel Conte
Our Lady of the Rocks
BOAT
Kotor
2
0 km 2
0 miles 2

7 DAYS

Day 1

Start your week-long Montenegrin adventure in the country's tourist hot spot, the Bay of Kotor. Here, the town of Herceg Novi is a lovely place to begin, its flower-scented promenade, Šetalište pet Danica, offering a relaxing morning amble. If you're looking for more of a challenge, the stiff climb up to the Spanish Fort leads to unbeatable views of the Adriatic. From town, it's less than an hour's drive around the bay to Risan (p83). Have a pitstop here to see its splendid Roman mosaics before continuing on to Perast (p44), where you can spend the rest of the day exploring this scenic spot.

Day 2

Half an hour's drive from Perast is Kotor, another of the bay's beautiful towns. Indulge in a low-key morning here, wandering the UNESCO-listed Old Town (p32), a delightful tangle of cobbled streets, Italianate squares and sumptuous palaces. In the afternoon, trek the hard yards along the town's formidable ramparts to Kotor Fortress,

well worth the sweat for its sweeping views. After your hike, reward yourself with Italian cuisine at Ladovina Kitchen and Wine Bar (p91), before a late-night glass of wine and spot of jazz at Jazz Club Evergreen (p90).

Day 3

Leaving Kotor behind, make your way along the steep, serpentine road to Lovćen National Park (p40), a magical moonscape of bleached limestone slopes and huge karst boulders; be sure to pay a visit to the mountaintop mausoleum of former prince-bishop Njegoš. If you've got some energy left, strike out on one of the park's great hikes, such as the relatively easy Wolf Trail. This circular loop begins at the Hotel Ivanov Konak (ivanovakorita.com), conveniently a great place to rest up for the night.

Sunbathing on the beach in Herceg Novi

Day 4

Not far from Lovćen lies Cetinje (p46), the unassuming former royal capital. It's packed with weighty museums, the best of which is King Nikola's Palace (p52), former home of Montenegro's only monarch. In the afternoon, head out to Lipa Cave (p105), located just outside town. Montenegro's premier show cave is packed with all kinds of formations, such as stalagmites.

Day 5

From Cetinje, sweep north to Durmitor (p22), a stunning drive into the heart of Montenegro's mightiest mountains. Upon arrival, it's time for serious thrills 'n' spills with whitewater rafting on the Tara River. Yearning for more adrenaline-fuelled fun? You can zip-line across the canyon, too. After a day of activities, an evening meal of oven-baked lamb in milk at Javorovaca (Javorovača bb), in the buzzy town of Žabljak (p116), is just the ticket.

Day 6

Start your penultimate day with a morning trek – Lokvice is doable in a couple of hours, but if you're after a

EAT
Located on the road from Cetinje to Lipa Cave is the Restoran Belveder (p109), an iconic local spot serving traditional Montenegrin cuisine. Try to get a seat on the scenic terrace (which overlooks the lush surrounding landscape).

longer, sterner test, the five-hour round trip to the Durmitor Ice Cave is the one to aim for. Take lunch back in Žabljak, before a somewhat more relaxing afternoon cooling off in the Black Lake (Crno Jezero; p113); if swimming's not your thing, you can hire a rowing boat from the Crno Jezero Restaurant, which is otherwise a lovely spot to grab a drink, chill and take in the scenery.

Day 7

Leaving Žabljak, the road heads east to Biogradska Gora National Park (p113), a land of ancient virgin forest, mountain pasture and glacial lakes. Pack a picnic and spend your final morning exploring this lovely landscape. Looking for more adventure? It's a two-hour drive south to Lake Skadar (p22), another of Montenegro's epic national parks and a beautiful place to end your trip.

Beautiful mountain scenery in Durmitor National Park

TOP 10 HIGHLIGHTS

Ostrog Monastery

EXPLORE THE
HIGHLIGHTS

There are some sights in Montenegro you simply shouldn't miss, and it's these attractions that make the Top 10. Discover what makes each one a must-see on the following pages.

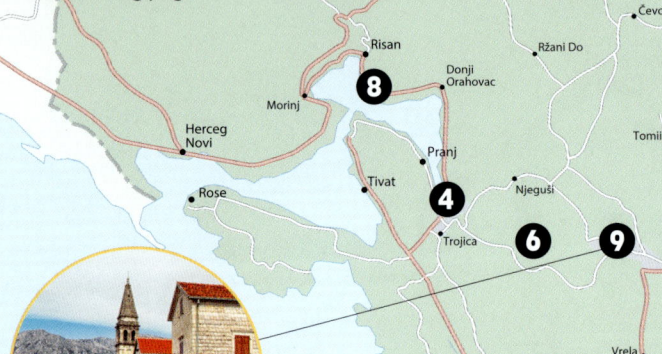

❶ Durmitor National Park

❷ Lake Skadar

❸ Budva

❹ Kotor Old Town

❺ Stari Bar

❻ Lovćen National Park

❼ Ulcinj

❽ Perast

❾ Cetinje

❿ Ostrog Monastery

Map labels: Bijele Poljane, Čevo, Ržani Do, Risan, Donji Orahovac, Tomil, Morinj, Herceg Novi, Pranj, Rose, Tivat, Trojica, Njeguši, Vrela, Obzovica, Seoca, Sveti Stefan, Petrovac na Moru

0 kilometres 10
0 miles 10

10

1

Zeta

Morača

Lopate

Veruša

Bolesestra

Ubli

Blizna

Klopot

Beovo

Smokovac

Podgorica

Dinoša

Zagora

Meterizi

Tuzi

Rijeka
Crnojevića

Bistrice

Komarno

Vranjina

2

Brijege

Virpazar

Seoca

*Lake
Skadar*

Mišii

Donji Murii

Sutomore

Tuemili

Šušanj

5

Martii

Shkodër

*Adriatic
Sea*

ALBANIA

Vladimir

Bushat

Bratica-
Braticë

7

Pistula-Pistullë

DURMITOR NATIONAL PARK

K3 Vuka Karadžića, Žabljak; durmitornp.com

Famed for its rugged peaks, glacial lakes and cavernous canyons (including Europe's deepest), UNESCO-protected Durmitor National Park is Montenegro's adventure capital. Endless outdoor activities are on offer here – from skiing to snowboarding, cycling to climbing – with much of the action based around the welcoming town of Žabljak.

1 Žabljak

Most visitors to Durmitor National Park stay in the tourism hub of Žabljak (p116). Destroyed during World War II, this small town has since been rebuilt and now hosts the area's best range of accommodation, alongside some great local restaurants.

2 Crno Jezero

Of Durmitor's 18 glacial lakes, Crno Jezero, or Black Lake (p113), is the largest. It's also one of the most popular, thanks to its accessible location (a short walk from Žabljak) and easy shoreline hiking trails. Wild swimmers flock here in the summer, but if you don't fancy a dip, rowing boats are available to hire instead.

> **TOP TIP**
>
> The entrance fee to the park can be paid at the ticket booth near Crno Jezero.

3 Tito's Cave

The former leader of Yugoslavia used numerous caves as hideouts during World War II. This shelter, near Crno Jezero, is just one of them. Historians believe the leader finalized his plans for the notorious Battle of Sutjeska here.

Rowing boats on scenic Crno Jezero

4 Bobotov Kuk
One of Montenegro's tallest peaks, and the highest mountain in Durmitor, Bobotov Kuk (*p59*) reaches a hulking 2,523 m (8,278 ft). It was first discovered by a mountaineering fraternity in the late 1800s and now attracts experienced hikers, who make the trek from Žabljak.

5 Unique Flora
Josif Pančić, father of Serbian botany, discovered numerous rare and endemic species native to Durmitor in the 1800s. One was the Durmitor violet, which can only be found in the park. Visitors should also keep a lookout for colourful species such as the Balkan primrose and Alpine rose.

6 Tara River Canyon
Only the most attractive section of this steep-sided natural wonder (*p113*) lies within Durmitor National Park – Tara is, after all, the deepest canyon in Europe. Beyond the superlatives, it draws

VIEW
You'll get epic views of the canyon from the Đurđevića Tara Bridge, but to see it from a different angle, hop in a raft instead.

The monumental Đurđevića Tara Bridge

thrill-seekers for its epic whitewater rafting.

7 Đurđevića Tara Bridge
Opened back in 1940, this incredible feat of engineering (*p116*) spans the Tara River. It's just as dramatic as the canyon it crosses, with huge concrete archways rising 172 m (564 ft) high above the water. Visitors can walk the length of the bridge, but be mindful that cars also cross it and the pavement is narrow.

8 Zminje Jezero
Tucked away amid plentiful pine forest, this lake rewards visitors with its emerald-green waters. It's a quieter option to Crno Jezero but lacks any amenities, so be sure to pack a picnic. While Zminje Jezero may translate to Snake Lake, this is the result of a local legend – visitors are very unlikely to see snakes around here today.

9 Ledena Pecina
Accessible via a challenging but beautiful hike, the Ice Cave hides inside the 2,164-m- (7,100-ft-) high peak of Obla Glava, on the south side of Bobotov Kuk. As the name suggests, it's filled with towers of ice and snow.

10 Rare Wildlife
Durmitor's status as Montenegro's largest and oldest national park, protected since 1952, has allowed endangered species such as the Balkan lynx, brown bears and peregrine falcons to survive and even thrive here.

A brown bear, resident of the park

Outdoor Activities

1. Skiing
The ski resort of Savin Kuk offers 5 km (3 miles) of snowy slopes and six lifts to transport you to heights of up to 2,200 m (6,900 ft). The journey there can be as dramatic as the glide down. Expect quality snow December to April.

2. Snowboarding
This sport came late to Durmitor but is now firmly established, with separate slopes at Savin Kuk designated to snowboarders, and rentals available.

3. Walking
Many trails wind through Durmitor but particularly memorable in the winter is the loop of 4 km (2.5 miles) around the frozen Crno Jezero. This scenic 90-minute walk can be extended an extra 6 km (4 miles) around Zminje Jezero.

4. Hiking
Depending on how challenging you want your hike to be – Bobotov Kuk is a gruelling seven hours, the last 20 minutes nothing short of onerous – Durmitor has routes to suit all levels. Stop by the visitor centre for tips.

5. Cycling
The Durmitor Ring *(p118)* has been designed for cyclists to take in the most dramatic panoramas around the park.

Whitewater rafting on the choppy Tara River

6. Whitewater Rafting
Thanks to the cascading waters that cut through Europe's deepest canyon (Tara), rafting here is second-to-none. It's best in summer and Durmitor Adventure *(durmitoradventure.com)* is a go-to operator.

7. Horse Riding
Within easy reach of Žabljak, Wild Beauty Adventure *(wildbeauty adventure.com)* offers horse-riding tours of between two hours and a whole day, around Vrazje Jezero or the slopes of Sinjajevina.

8. Zip-lining
If the Tara Zip Line with Montenegro Adventure Travel *(montenegro adventure.travel)* – a minute's worth of 120 km/h (75 mph) thrills from the Đurđevića Tara Bridge – is a bit too extreme for you, try the gentler Red Rock line. It's also near the bridge.

9. Kayaking
Summer is the ideal time to hire a kayak and head out over the shimmering waters of the Black Lake – boats can be hired near the lake for just a few euros.

10. Climbing
Durmitor's craggy mountains are great for climbing, and none more so than Prutaš. This photogenic peak promises climbing routes of varying difficulty – plus incredible views. Routes are best tackled in late spring with Funky Tours *(funkytours.com)*.

Off-road cycling through Durmitor National Park

Frozen towers of varying sizes in the Ice Cave, formed beneath the mountain of Obla Glava in Durmitor National Park

THE LANDSCAPE OF DURMITOR

With its 18 glacial lakes (called "mountain eyes" by the locals), numerous caves (including the country's deepest), rugged peaks and swooping, verdant valleys, Durmitor National Park is home to Montenegro's most dramatic scenery. This rich geographical landscape has formed as a result of the area's changing geology. The Durmitor massif is largely made up of limestone and dolomite rock, which became particularly porous during the Devonia geological era. As the bedrock began to dissolve, karstification occured, changing the landscape and forming large sinkholes and caves. That's the science, and it's on full show in the park today – particularly in Durmitor's caves, which are pin-pricked with stalactites and stalagmites. Spelunkers have any number of these gaping holes to tackle, but the most fascinating is arguably the Ice Cave (Ledena Pecina; *p23*). Hidden in the mountain of Obla Glava, it's a poster-child for the park's unique and awe-inspiring landscape.

A glacial lake backdropped by a jagged mountain peak, two aspects of Durmitor National Park's thrilling geological landscape

LAKE SKADAR

📍 E4 ⓘ Virpazar; nparkovi.me

The largest lake in southern Europe, Skadar forms the border between Montenegro and Albania. Protected on either side as a National Park and Managed Nature Reserve, the lake is a haven of freshwater biodiversity, with 280 types of bird, including rare Dalmatian pelicans.

1 Boat Tours
Whether you want to gaze at ruins on abandoned islands or spot an array of local bird-life, the best way to explore Skadar is by boat. English-speaking local guides can be hired from Kingfisher Boat and Kayak *(skadarlakeboat cruise.com)*, based in Virpazar, the main town in the area.

2 Virpazar
The gateway town to Lake Skadar, pretty Virpazar *(p98)* straddles the Crmnica River that feeds into Lake Skadar. It's a popular holiday spot, and the setting-off point for boat tours around the lake.

3 Lesendro
Visible from the Belgrade–Bar railway line that skirts the lake, this island fortress provided Montenegrins with temporary respite from the invading Ottomans in the 1830s. The stronghold eventually fell, however, and is now in ruins.

4 Skanderbeg
An unusual lake resident, this sunken Habsburg-era passenger steamer can be seen in the Bay of Karuč when the water levels are low – it lies in reasonably good condition at 10 m (36 ft) below the surface.

5 Karuč
This waterfront community was created by fishers, who built huts overlooking the reedy waters. Life here still revolves around the lake, with numerous rustic restaurants serving grilled fish. The village is also home to the house where one of the prince-bishops of Montenegro, Petar I Petrović-Njegoš, once wintered.

6 Swimming
Fed by karst springs, Lake Skadar is one of Montenegro's best freshwater swimming spots. Many boat trips around the lake end with a splash in the water (so be sure to pack your towel).

7 Beška
The name of both the island and the

> ### 🍴 EAT
> Overlooking the scenic Karuč waterfront, the family-run Restoran Kod Aca-Karuč *(Karuc bb)* serves up tasty grilled fish and local wine.

Religious buildings atop Beška island

Swimming among the lake's lily pads

restored medieval monastery upon it, Beška features two churches from the early 1400s (St George's and St Mary's), today overseen by the Serbian Orthodox Church. St Mary's contains the remains of Jelena Balšić, a princess from the noble dynasty who was responsible for the church's construction. The sweeping views of the lake from the island are stunning.

8 Murići Beach
Looking out towards the former monastic island retreat of Beška, Murići (p100) is a rare sandy beach on the Skadar shoreline. Join locals here for an afternoon of swimming and sunbathing; surprisingly, it's never too crowded.

9 Kayaking
Those looking to go it alone (rather than join a boat tour) can hire kayaks at Virpazar. Visitors are given equipment, including a lifejacket, instructions and safety briefing, then left to explore the waters, shoreline and islands for a set period of time, from an hour to a day. Kingfisher (skadar lakeboatcruise.com) is a go-to hire company.

10 Grmožur
Just offshore of Virpazar, this rugged islet became a fortified prison after the Montenegrin-Ottoman War of the 1870s. While the prison's stone walls are now in ruins, the island has found a new lease of life as a wildlife haven. Local birds, including the famous Dalmatian pelican, nest here, and snakes are frequently spotted slithering in the rugged undergrowth.

TOP TIP

The best times for bird-watching are early morning and late afternoon.

A flock of pelicans in the reeds around Lake Skadar

Birdlife on Lake Skadar

1. Dalmatian Pelicans
Spotting one of the world's largest freshwater birds is the highlight of any ornithological tour. The symbol of Skadar itself, the Dalmatian pelican is graceful in flight despite weighing some 10 kg (22 pounds).

2. Great Cormorants
Often seen perched atop rocks ready to dive for fish, these large black birds make for a dramatic sight as they plunge into the water.

3. Eurasian Coots
Common on Lake Skadar, these bulky black birds rarely take flight but rather splash in ungainly fashion across the water. Visitors should be prepared to hear their noisy calls at night if they stay by the lake.

4. Great-crested Grebes
Nesting in platforms among the reeds, these swift, graceful creatures gain their bright plumage during the breeding season, when elaborate courtship displays take place. Expert fishers, they hunt their prey underwater.

5. Squacco Herons
Wintering in Africa and breeding in southern Europe, these tawny-brown birds seem to change colour when they fly; in fact it's just their stark white wings (usually hidden) that suddenly appear.

6. Alpine Swifts
These speedy migratory birds spend an inordinate amount of time in the air, catching insects in flight. You'll usually see them flying over the lake on late summer evenings.

7. Common Terns
Longer-billed than their Arctic cousins, these grey-and-white birds gather in noisy flocks above Lake Skadar in late summer, before commencing their annual trek to the tropical south.

8. Short-toed Snake Eagles
Named by the ancient Greeks, these brown-and-white birds of prey are found in ever-decreasing numbers in this part of Europe. They return here in spring after wintering in sunny sub-Saharan Africa.

9. Little Egrets
Typically seen stalking their prey in shallow lake water, these bright-white birds have long black beaks and spindly legs. They're smaller cousins of the heron and nest in colonies within the reeds.

10. Eastern Black-eared Wheatears
Distinguished by their striking black-and-white colour pattern and rapid birdsong, these diminutive birds breed at the lake before heading south to Sudan for the winter.

A common tern hovering above lily pads at Lake Skadar

CONSERVATION EFFORTS

With 280 bird species recorded around the lake, plus 48 types of endemic fish, Lake Skadar is arguably Montenegro's most important wildlife reserve. Its status has been recognized by both its border countries: it is protected as a Managed Nature Reserve on the Albanian side and as a National Park on its Montenegro side (the latter status granted in 1982). Two specific areas of the lake (Panceva Oka and Manastirska Tapija) are specially protected within this remit and largely off-limits to tourists, therefore allowing cormorants, egrets and herons to nest undisturbed around the water. The ongoing EU-funded, cross-border project Lake Skadar Without Chemical Pollution also adds another layer of protection for the lake's residents, as it aims to control the flow of wastewater. Yet tourism is on the rise, with bird-watchers providing essential income to local residents. And while accommodation options near the lake are still limited to a scattering of guesthouses, plans for further development have certainly ruffled the feathers of environmental groups and Virpazar residents.

The islet of Grmožur, a popular nesting area for birdlife

BUDVA

◉ C4 🏠 Trg Sunca 1, Budva; budva.travel

Attracting the lion's share of visitors to the region, the seaside resort of Budva represents the Montenegrin coast at its liveliest. While its Old Town has plenty of historical landmarks (including a formidable citadel), it's Budva's sweeping sandy beaches and lively bar and restaurant scene that really draw the crowds here.

2 Citadel
A medieval strong-hold constructed in the 9th century, Budva's citadel was later fortified and expanded by the Venetians to curb the encroaching threat of Ottoman invasion. Built on a hill overlooking the Adriatic, the building now features a compact museum dedicated to Budva's maritime past.

3 Mogren Beach
Named after a Spanish sailor who washed ashore here in the 14th century, Mogren Beach consists of two fine shingle bays inter-linked by a tunnel.

4 St Ivan Church
This Roman Catholic church was built in the 7th century and later altered by the Venetians, who constructed new features including the lofty bell tower. Inside, it houses impressive Greek and Venetian frescoes and relics, test-ament to the various empires that have laid claim to Budva.

5 Church of the Holy Trinity
An exterior of striped honey- and pink-coloured stone marks one of the country's more unusual churches (p54). Built after the collapse of the

1 Stari Grad
The jewel of coastal Montenegro, Budva's photo-worthy Old Town rivals Dubrovnik for its polished marble streets and Venetian-era fort-ifications. It's been con-tinuously inhabited since the 5th century BCE, when it was founded as a Greek colony. Today, it's packed with popular restaurants and bars, many catering to tourists.

Historic Podostrog Monastery

Venetian Republic, this Orthodox church features a kaleidoscopic display of Byzantine frescoes inside.

6 Sveti Nikola

As you glide on the Adriatic to Montenegro's largest sea island, its Jurassic qualities (picture limestone peaks covered in lush vegetation) fall into view. But it's the rocky coves most sunbathers come for. Note that the uninhabited island (known locally as Školj) can only be visited on day trips.

7 Podostrog Monastery

🏠 78 Mainshi put

Accessed via an uphill hike from Podmaine Monastery, the fortified

A shingle beach fringing Budva's Old Town

Podostrog Monastery was the former residence of Montenegro's *vladikas* (prince-bishops) – the most famous, Petar II Petrović Njegoš (*p41*), wrote his epic *The Mountain Wreath* here. The site has various churches from the 12th and 18th centuries to explore.

8 Museum of the City of Budva

🏠 11 Petra I Petrovića

After the 1979 earthquake, archaeologists unearthed a raft of important artifacts, particularly around Budva's citadel. Many of them are now contained in this museum. Housed in a 19th-century building, it features some 450 exhibits, spanning Greek, Roman, Byzantine and Slavic history.

9 Ballerina Statue

Inspired by the local legend of a disappearing sailor and his grief-stricken fiancée, who spent her remaining days gazing at the open sea, sculptor Gradimir Aleksić's statue is a local symbol of Budva. Located on the coastal walkway to Mogren

Beach, it's a popular spot for visitors to take photos and imitate her graceful dance, suspended mid-air and backdropped by the sea.

10 Sveti Stefan

Connected to the mainland by a thin tombolo, the islet of Sveti Stefan (*p95*) is a 15th-century fishing village, a few miles south of Budva. Owned by a luxury hotel (which is temporarily closed), the islet is currently off-limits to visitors. However, you can still enjoy the view from the scenic sandy beaches along the coastline.

Gradimir Aleksić's elegant Ballerina

KOTOR OLD TOWN

◉ B3 ℹ Trg od Oružja; kotor.travel

Sitting at the end of a long bay, Kotor is one of the Adriatic coast's best-preserved old towns. Over 2,500 years old, it's been ruled by many different groups, including the Roman, Byzantine and First French empires, with the Venetian Republic making a big impact on its architecture. Today, it's a UNESCO World Heritage Site twice over for its Venetian fortifications and its Venetian historic centre.

1 Rector's Palace
Until Napoleon arrived in 1806, this was the spot from which Venice ruled Montenegro's Adriatic coast. It's now part of the Hotel Cattaro, but it's still possible to step inside to admire its striking Venetian architecture.

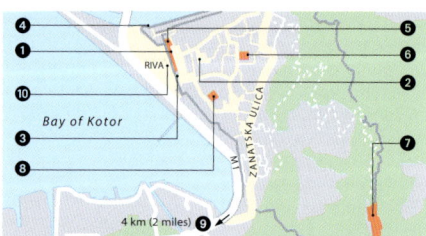

2 Cat Museum
Kotor's streets are home to many stray cats, so it's no surprise that there's a niche museum dedicated to felines here (p53). Browse its cat-focused collection, made up of prints, manuscripts and vintage magazines.

3 Sea Gate
Three defensive gates built by the Venetians enclose the Old Town: the Gurdić Gate (p34), the River Gate and the Sea Gate. The walls near the latter feature a beautiful carving of the winged Lion of St Mark.

4 Kampana Tower
For visitors arriving to Kotor by boat, this squat tower is the first thing they see. Built in the 14th century as a defensive structure to protect the Old Town, its bell-like shape was designed to deflect attacking cannonballs.

Kotor's scenic Old Town, illuminated at dusk

5 Napoleon's Theatre

One of the Balkans' first playhouses, this theatre was first opened by Napoleon's forces in 1810. Later used as the Town Hall, it is now part of the Hotel Cattaro.

6 Maritime Museum

Housed in a heritage palace from the late 1800s, this museum (p52) showcases the fascinating naval history of Montenegro. Inside, three floors are filled with maritime models, maps, instruments and weaponry.

> **SHOP**
> Next to the Maritime Museum, Antiques Stanković (69 326 989) is a gold mine of treasures, including coins and naval instruments.

7 Kotor Fortress

It may be a ruin (p69) but what's left of the stronghold of Roman Emperor Justinian is still worth exploring. It's 1,350 steps to the top of the fortress (also known as St John's Fortress), but the panoramic views are incredible.

8 Gallery of Solidarity

🏠 Ulica 2 w muzeji kotor.me

Artists and sculptors, mainly from the former Yugoslavia, exhibit in this 17th-century palace, once home to the literary Pima family.

9 Kotor Cable Car

Taking 11 minutes to ascend, the Kotor cable car (p88) provides plenty of time to take in the views over the town, bay and surrounding hills.

> **CRUISE SHIPS**
> As Montenegro's tourism industry has developed in the 21st century, the country has seen an increase in the number of cruise ships visiting Kotor, with hordes of tourists flooding into town. Websites such as CruiseMapper (cruisemapper.com) indicate the arrival and departure times of each ship, so you can plan ahead to avoid the crowds.

10 Trg od Oružja

Given the town's combative past, it's little surprise that the name of its main square translates as "Arms Square". A highlight here is the clock tower (p34).

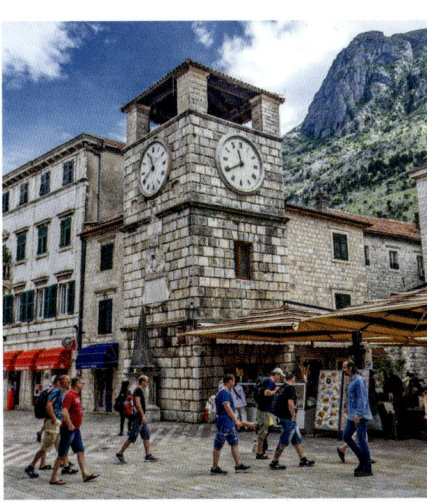

The clock tower in Trg od Oružja

Kotor Old Town's Architecture

The imposing exterior of the Cathedral of St Tryphon

1. Cathedral of St Tryphon

Consecrated in 1166, Kotor's cathedral (p54) was devastated by two earthquakes, in 1667 and 1979. Since restored, this striking building has two Baroque bell towers and a Romanesque interior, complete with a vaulted roof. Other highlights include Baroque frescoes and a gilded altar.

2. Clock Tower

🄰 Trg od Oružja

Built in the 17th century, Kotor's boxy clock tower – which stands guard over the main square of Trg od Oružja (p33) – blends both Baroque and Gothic architectural styles.

3. Church of St Nicholas

🄰 Ulica 1

This church was built in the Serbo-Byzantine style in the early 1900s, when Kotor was under Habsburg rule. While the exterior of this ecclesiastical building is rather plain, there's a wealth of golden iconography inside.

4. Bizanti Palace

🄰 Stari Grad 327

Dating back to the 1300s, this imposing landmark is a mixture of Renaissance and Baroque styles.

5. Lombardic Palace

🄰 Just off Trg Sv Luke

This robust property was built in the Baroque style in the mid-1700s, with balconies framed by stone balustrades. It hosted the Russian consulate during Kotor's brief Napoleonic era.

6. Beskuća Palace

🄰 Just off Trg od Oružja

This property was built by maritime traders in 1776, shortly before Venice lost control of the area. Within its striking Gothic portal is a coat of arms dominated by the winged Lion of Venice.

7. Grubonja Palace

This 17th-century palace was home to the local Grubonja family. It's recognizable by its snake-themed plaque at the front of the building.

8. Venetian fortifications

The Illryians first built fortifications in Kotor, but it was the Venetians who gave the structures much of their current appearance. Look out for carvings of the Lion of St Mark on the ramparts for proof of Venetian construction.

9. Drago Palace

🄰 Pjaca Sv Tripuna

Home to the Regional Institute for Cultural Preservation, this building neatly captures Kotor's architectural heritage: Gothic before the earthquake of 1667, partly Baroque after.

10. Gurdić Gate

🄰 Ulica 2

At the southern end of the Old Town, the Gurdić Gate – a defensive system of passages and drawbridges – was built between the 1200s and 1700s.

A section of Kotor's fortifications, which were bolstered during the Venetian Republic

THE VENETIAN INFLUENCE

When under the control of the Venetian Republic, Kotor belonged to Venetian Albania, which was – unlike its name suggests – mainly located in modern-day Montenegro. The Venetians managed to control the area for nearly four centuries (from 1420 until 1797) despite occasionally being attacked by the Ottomans. This long period of rule had a profound impact on Kotor and the wider area. For one thing, it's estimated that more than 60 per cent of locals spoke Venetian at the time, albeit with regional differences. For another, Venetian control led to a boom in arts and culture, especially during the Renaissance. Kotor was particularly famous for its poets, including Ludovico Pasquali and Giovanni Bona de Boliris, who were both born and bred in the town; the latter's *Ode to Cattaro* lauded Kotor. While Kotor lost some of its Venetian cultural heritage when under Habsburg rule, Venice's impact on the town can still be seen in its architecture, especially the town's imposing fortifications and palaces.

Illustration of historic Kotor, a town ruled by numerous empires, most prominently the Venetian Republic

STARI BAR

📍 D5 🌐 starigradbar.com

Nestled on the edge of the Dinaric Mountains among rolling olive groves, Stari Bar was once a bustling town, but was devastated by the earthquake of 1979. Today, its walled centre (featuring some 250 historic structures) is largely in a state of ruin, though some buildings have been restored to their former glory.

1 The Customs House

One of the country's best examples of Renaissance architecture, this building was constructed in the 15th century by the Venetians. Located on the edge of the Stari Bar Fortress, it's a great place to start exploring, with a small museum explaining the site's complex history.

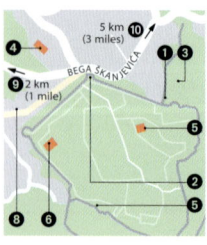

2 Stari Bar Fortress

One of the town's most impressive sights, the fortress is home to centuries of history, with a mixture of churches, mosques and towers contained within its walls. The €2 entrance fee includes access to a small museum.

3 Bar Aqueduct

A feat of Ottoman engineering, this bridge once transported water from the mountains down to the town. Today, it's the last remaining aqueduct in Montenegro, with 17 arches rising above a deep ravine, surrounded by tawny mountains.

4 Omerbašića Mosque

Just outside the main gate of Stari Bar, this rectangular mosque, built in 1662, features a simple minaret. Near the entrance lies the mausoleum of Hasan, a local Dervish.

5 Ottoman Heritage Sites

Other Ottoman heritage sites in Stari Bar are evidence of this empire's 300-year-long rule. Highlights include the Turkish Powder Mill, which houses a *lapidarium* (a gallery of stone monuments) and a traditional Turkish bathhouse from the 17th or 18th century.

*Looking towards
the ruins of Stari Bar*

6 The Bishops Palace

Known locally as Kuća Omerbašić, after the last family who resided here, the former residence of the town's archbishop has been converted into an archaeology museum. Inside is a modest collection of objects found on local digs, including pottery and ceramics.

7 Stari Bar Churches

There are 10 churches in Stari Bar, although few remain intact. St John's Church stands out, having been entirely rebuilt by a local family with links to the original church. Two others of note are the 14th-century St Verenada's and the 15th-century St Catherine's (undergoing restoration).

8 Gradska Carsija

The souvenir shops lining the cobblestoned Gradska Carsija sell local wine, olive oil and rakia. Look out for Gavodalla, which contains a colourful display of handmade Montenegrin ceramics.

9 Stara Maslina

Not far from Stari Bar, in the village of Tomba, this 2,000-year-old olive tree *(p97)* is one of the oldest in the world. A local symbol of peace, it pre-dates any recorded history of Stari Bar itself. There's a small entrance fee to see it.

10 Mount Rumija

A short drive from town is Mount Rumija. Its 1,600-m (5,200-ft) peak can be reached via a challenging climb, which traverses the villages of Velembusi and Baltina, passes by an Orthodox church and winds through forests. From the summit there are extraordinary views of Stari Bar's ruins, olive groves and, in the distance, the turquoise Adriatic Sea.

STARI BAR'S PAST

The town's strategic location, close to the coast and backed by mountains, made it a tantalizing prize. First settled by the Romans, it later fell under Venetian and Ottoman rule, before returning to Montenegrin hands in 1877. Although Stari Bar was abandoned after the 1979 earthquake, attempts to restore parts of the town are now underway.

*Clockwise from right
A mural on one of Stari Bar's ruins; the Ottoman-built aqueduct; Stara Maslina, an ancient olive tree*

A cobbled street outside Stari Bar's ruined walled centre

LOVĆEN NATIONAL PARK

C3 🔲 nparhovi.me/parhs/lovcen

Integral to Montenegro's national identity, Lovćen is both the "black mountain" that inspired the country's name and a national park of dense forest, rare flora and dramatic slopes. Atop its famous peak, surveying the nation, the mausoleum of Petar II Petrović-Njegoš contains the remains of the country's great poet and powerful ruler.

1 Kotor Cable Car

Connecting the coastal resort of Kotor with the slopes of Lovćen National Park, this spectacular ride (p88) provides panoramic views of the peaks and access to the area's hiking trails.

2 Njeguši

You might not think it from the simple stone cottages, but this tiny settlement (p107) on the slopes of Mount Lovćen was once the seat of the prominent Petrović dynasty (1697–1918).

3 Njeguši Pršut

Wherever you dine around the Lovćen National Park, this particular variety of air-dried, wood-smoked prosciutto (p72) will be on the menu. It's best sampled on a platter with local cheese, fresh bread and a glass of Vranac wine.

4 Alpine Coaster

Within easy reach of the upper terminal of the Kotor cable car, this vertigo-inducing rollercoaster speeds along the slopes of Lovćen to offer fantastic views of the sea and the park. It's a thrilling 1-km- (0.5-mile-) long ride.

5 Hiking Mount Lovćen

The eponymous mountain actually consists of two peaks, Štirovnik and Jezerski Vrh. The former is higher but Jezerski Vrh is more popular (it's topped by the famous Njegoš mausoleum). Maps showing other hikes are available at the park's visitor centre.

> ✳ **EAT**
> Want to try some of Njeguši's famous prosciutto? Make a beeline for Kafana Kod Pera Na Bukovicu (hodpera. com), a traditional restaurant in Njeguši.

Sweeping views from atop Mount Lovćen

The entrance to the Njegoš Mausoleum

varieties such as the small, perennial Lovćen bell. Expert tour guides can be arranged at the park's visitor centre if contacted ahead of time.

6 Njegoš Mausoleum

Conceived by the eminent Croatian sculptor Ivan Meštrović, the last resting place of Montenegro's great poet and 19th-century ruler, Petar II Petrović-Njegoš, is dramatically set atop Mount Lovćen. Visitors can enter the mausoleum for a small fee.

7 Botany Tours

Once dauntingly remote, Lovćen is home to some 1,300 species of plants, including local

8 Adventure Park Lovćen

🏠 Poda

Visiting Lovćen with the family? Head to this outdoor attraction for a fun day out. Consisting of rope trails high-up in the trees, each with a number of obstacles, the course is designed to test everyone from five years old and up.

9 Ivanova Korita

🌐 ivanovakorita.com

Once the villa of King Nikola, this historic building has been converted into a complex of rustic lodges. Located on Lovćen's southern slopes, the site also features sports courts, a garden and picnic area, popular with passing hikers.

PETAR II PETROVIĆ-NJEGOŠ

His status underlined by the mausoleum atop Mount Lovćen, Petar II Petrović-Njegoš was one of the country's most influential rulers, and a revered writer who propagated the notion of a south Slav state. When this became Yugoslavia, nearly 70 years after his death in 1851, Njegoš was honoured as its national poet.

10 Fortress Goražda

🏠 Shaljari

Guarding the ancient capital of Cetinje and observing any movement in the Bay of Kotor below, this Habsburg-built stronghold sits just beyond the edge of Lovćen National Park. It's free to enter.

ULCINJ

E6 ⓘ Majke Tereze bb (Zgrada Idea Market); ulcinj.travel

Montenegro's most southerly town, this seaside resort is a popular spot with holidaymakers, including those from nearby Albania (it's not too far to the border). The town is most famous for its historic Old Town and plethora of beaches, including the sweeping Velika Plaža (Big Beach) and women-only Ladies' Beach.

1 Ulcinj Old Town
Built by the Greeks, and later fortified by the Romans, Ulcinj's walled Old Town sits above the Adriatic Sea. Within its fortified walls is a veritable parade of medieval, Venetian and Ottoman architecture, painstakingly restored after the 1979 earthquake.

2 St Nicholas's Church
Built in 1890 following the end of Ottoman rule, this Serbian-Orthodox church is a comparatively recent addition to Ulcinj. Found just below the main gate of the Old Town, it occupies the site of a 15th-century monastery and is surrounded by spindly olive trees.

3 Balšić Tower
Soaring above the Old Town, this impressive citadel-fortress was built by the Balšić dynasty in the late 14th century. The Ottomans later added a third floor, plus the spherical dome on the ground floor.

4 Pasha's Mosque
Perhaps the most striking of Ulcinj's six mosques, thanks to its elegant Ottoman-era design and lofty minaret, this building was constructed by locals using materials looted from stolen Venetian ships. A traditional hammam lies inside, the first of its kind in Montenegro.

Pasha's mosque, with its green-tipped minaret

Ulcinj's historic
Old Town

dedicated to those who fought in World War II – is perched above Mala Plaža. Though now weathered and graffiti-scrawled, the Futurist sculpture, which features two V-shaped white wings that resemble crashed fighter planes, is still worth lingering over.

8 Buzuku Montenegro Olive Oil Farm

Just outside Ulcinj, this family-run farm offers an insight into the area's olive oil production. On guided tours, visitors can admire the more than a millennia-old olive trees, learn how extra virgin olive oil is made and enjoy a tasting session.

9 Velika Plaža

The longest stretch of sand on the Adriatic coast, this 12-km (7-mile) Big Beach draws the crowds. During summer, visitors come to laze on

5 Ladies' Beach

This secluded cove is exclusively for women. It owes this status to the purported healing properties of its dark-green waters, which contain a high level of sulphur – said to be a natural treatment for infertility. It's a clothing-optional spot (many locals swim naked here).

6 Sapore di Mare

When Mala Plaža, another of Ulcinj's many beaches, becomes too busy, head over to this shady cove nearby. While there's no sand, it offers a more peaceful experi-ence for swimming and sunbathing. There's also an oceanside seafood restaurant and bar, the excellent Sapore di Mare *(382 69 814 742)*.

7 Freedom Monument

This striking *spomenik* – a Socialist-era monument

> **DRINK**
> Rigo Bar *(Rr Hafiz Ali Ulqinaku)* is a go-to in Ulcinj thanks to its barista-quality coffee, afford-able cocktails and weekend DJ sets on the terrace.

its soft sands or try kite- or windsurfing; it's a great spot for both, thanks to a westerly breeze.

10 Ada Bojana

This pretty island is located at the south-ern end of Big Beach, at the mouth of the Bojana River. As well as being a popular naturist colony, it has a beautiful sandy beach, a cluster of excel-lent seafood restaurants and, for those staying the night, waterside treehouses to rent.

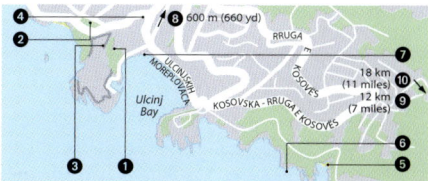

8

PERAST

📍 B2 ℹ️ Mjesna Zajednica, Perast 2; perast.com

A historical rival to nearby Kotor, scenic Perast was once a hive of maritime activity, especially during the 17th and 18th centuries. Evidence of its seafaring wealth is still clear to see: spot the dazzling captains' palaces and gorgeous churches – Our Lady of the Rocks is arguably the most famous – still standing today.

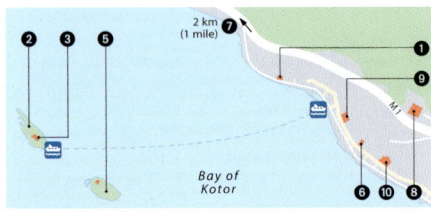

1 Perast Museum

🏛️ Obala Marka Martinovića bb

The town museum focuses on local maritime heritage, with items on display including charts, costumes and weaponry. It occupies the magnificent Baroque Bujović Palace, which guards the entrance to Perast and was financed by the seamanship that earned Perast its reputation.

2 Our Lady of the Rocks

Two islets sit close to Perast: Our Lady of the Rocks (p84) and St George. The former is the most famous, an artificial island that was made by locals using boatloads of stones from the mainland. It is one of Perast's most photographed sights.

3 Our Lady of the Rocks Church

Found on Our Lady of the Rocks, this Catholic church houses a series of paintings by Baroque artist Tripo Kokolja. They depict the life of the Virgin, as inspired by local poet and theologian, Andrija Zmajević.

4 Fašinada

This traditional event takes place on 22 July each year. On the day, a convoy of small boats, festooned in greenery and loaded with stones, heads over to Our Lady of the Rocks. The rocks are deposited to help shore up the island, an activity that is followed by singing and feasting.

5 St George's Island

St George's (p87), the second of the islands near Perast, is a naturally formed islet. This pretty spot is dotted with cypress trees and home to a 12th-century Benedictine monastery that's notable for being the last resting place of many a sea captain.

The island of Our Lady of the Rocks

The seafaring town of Perast at sunset

TOP TIP

To visit the islands, hop on one of the frequent ferries running from the town's dock.

Banja was constructed in the 1720s on the ruins of an older religious building. Its name is a misnomer – this is a nunnery, whose present-day inhabitants sell healing herbs they collect nearby.

Perast. The site helped protect the town from invasion, especially an attempt by the Ottomans on 15 May 1654. Today, just two of the ten towers remain.

6 Brajković-Martinović Palace

This suitably imposing building sits near a row of busts depicting key maritime figures from Perast. Inside is a permanent exhibition that pays homage to the palace's two namesakes: Brajković, a flotilla captain, and Martinović, a nautical expert hired by Peter the Great to train cadets.

7 Banja Monastery

With a gorgeous location overlooking the waterfront outside Perast,

8 Church of St Nicholas

St Nicholas (*p54*) is, in fact, two churches: one was built in 1616, with the other half-completed through the 1700s. Most visitors come for the belfry, which offers wonderful views over Perast. It was designed by Hvar architect Ivan Škarpa.

9 Fort of the Holy Cross

Built on the site of an ancient church – hence its name – this Venetian stronghold was once part of an impressive ten-tower fortification system surrounding

10 Smekja Palace

The largest of Perast's palaces dates from 1764 when wealthy merchants began its construction. At the entrance is the insignia of the Smekja family, showing a hand holding the stalk of a date palm with stars. The third floor has fabulous panoramas across the town's scenic waterfront.

SHOP
Cattarissimo, next to St Nicholas, is an excellent ice-cream store offering lactose-free options, plus almond cake, a local speciality.

9

CETINJE

📍 C3 ℹ️ Bajova 2, Cetinje; cetinje.travel

Founded in the 15th century, Cetinje was Montenegro's royal capital until the country became part of Yugoslavia. While the title then passed to Podgorica, this picturesque town has remained the country's cultural centre – count the grand institutions, statues of national heroes and famed museums and you'll see why.

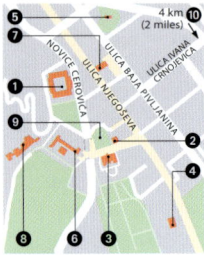

1 National Museum

🏛️ Novice Cerovića 🔗

Established in 1896, this is the largest museum in Montenegro and comprises a number of institutions. The site's History Museum and the Art Gallery of Montenegro are temporarily closed.

2 Ethnographic Museum

🏛️ Dvorski Trg 🔗

This fascinating museum (under the umbrella of the National Museum) showcases a broad collection of colourful folk costumes and local instruments.

3 King Nikola's Palace

Montenegro's most popular cultural site (p52) is set in the castle built for the Petrović-Njegoš dynasty in 1867. The permanent collection covers the period of Montenegrin statehood from the Middle Ages to 1918.

4 Plavi Dvorac

🏛️ Njegoševa

The official residence of the President of Montenegro was built in 1895 for the then heir, the Crown Prince Danilo. While you may not enter – unless you're a head of state – you can admire its impressive architecture from outside.

5 Vlaška Church

🏛️ Baja Pivljanina

This pretty Serbian Orthodox church is located on the northern edge

Clockwise from right
Interior of the Museum of King Nikola; scenic Cetinje Monastery; Lipa Cave; the National Museum

of Cetinje. It features two original *stećci* (ornate medieval tombstones) plus a guard rail made from the metal of Ottoman-era rifles.

6 Biljarda
🏠 Novice Cerovića

Named after his favourite pastime (the name translates to Billiard Palace), Petar II Petrović-Njegoš's *(p41)* former residence is dedicated to his life and literary output. Don't miss the original manuscript of his epic *The Mountain Wreath*.

7 Miodrag Dado Đurić Gallery
🏠 89 Njegoševa

This multifunctional contemporary gallery and arts space is named after the revered Montenegrin

Historic Vlaška Church, in northern Cetinje

artist Miodrag Đurić (nicknamed Dado). He died in 2010, two years before this gallery opened in his hometown.

8 Cetinje Monastery

Founded in 1484 and rebuilt in 1704, this seat of the Serbian Orthodox Church contains priceless Christian relics such as the mummified right hand of John the Baptist.

9 Monument to Ivan Crnojević

The statue of Cetinje's founder stands tall in a leafy park near the Billiard Palace. It was crafted in a modern style in the 1980s by local sculptor Ante Grzetic.

10 Lipa Cave

Just outside Cetinje and a popular excursion from town, Lipa Cave

(p105) is one of the country's most intriguing attractions. Within its gaping underground expanse is a dramatic array of towering stalactites and stalagmites, connected by walkways.

A ROYAL HISTORY

Founded in 1482 by ruler Ivan Crnojević, Cetinje was chosen for its defensible mountain location. It was largely rebuilt under the Petrović dynasty from 1697, and later flourished under Petar II Petrović-Njegoš in the 1800s. During the latter's reign, many of the town's stately institutions and elegant embassies were constructed.

OSTROG MONASTERY

📍 D1 ℹ️ Ivana Milutinovića 10; manastirostrog.com

A place of pilgrimage and a feat of engineering, the gravity-defying Ostrog Monastery dates back 350 years. First founded in the 17th century (and later renovated in the 20th century), it still operates as a house of worship. Its signature white façade carved into a sheer cliff face is arguably one of the country's most striking sights.

1 Upper Monastery
Ostrog's star attraction, the 17th-century Upper Monastery sits behind the shiny white façade (added in the 1920s after a fire). It contains two cave churches, full of stunning frescoes, and the bones of founder St Basil of Ostrog.

2 Frescoes
The most striking feature of the two cave churches in the Upper Monastery are the priceless frescoes created by Serbian master Radul, also responsible for the painted icons in Praskvica Monastery (p98). Their colours still shine, some 350 years after their creation.

3 Lower Monastery
Constructed around 150 years after its loftier counterpart, the more prosaic Lower Monastery was originally a tiny village. It was converted into a facility to serve the pilgrims in the Upper Monastery, with a granary, a church and housing.

4 Healing Spring
Many visit Ostrog with the hope of being cured of an ailment by miraculous means.

Colourful fresco in the Upper Monastery

Ostrog Monastery, carved into the cliff face

TOP TIP

It's best to visit the monastery first thing in the morning, before the crowds arrive.

Whether you're a believer or not, everyone can drink the water from the reputed healing spring by the Lower Monastery.

5 Shrine of St Basil

Ostrog Monastery is home to numerous holy sites, but the Shrine of St Basil is perhaps the most sacred. It contains the bones of the founding saint, wrapped in fabric and guarded by a solemn monk. The site is revered by locals and visitors are advised not to take photographs of the shrine.

6 Crkva Sv Trojice

The centrepiece of the Lower Monastery, the Church of the Holy Trinity was built around the same time, in 1824. A simple exterior hides a panoply of frescoes.

7 Crkva Sv Mučenika Stanka

Set between the Upper and Lower Monasteries, the Church of St Stanko the Martyr is known for both its vibrant frescoes, and gruesome backstory. It's named after a shepherd boy, Stanko, whose hands were chopped off when he failed to convert to Islam.

8 Danilovgrad

Surprisingly rich in attractions for a community of just 5,000 people, Danilovgrad is the nearest settlement to Ostrog Monastery. Its tranquil setting beside the winding Zeta river has attracted generations of artists.

9 Umjetnička Kolonija

⌂ Trg 9 Decembar

Established in 1972, Danilovgrad's art colony is particularly strong on sculpture (examples of which are dotted around the garden). The gallery also hosts an annual sculpture festival.

10 Zavičajni Muzej

⌂ Lazara Đurovića

Roman and medieval finds, along with artifacts from World War II, fill the Homeland Museum in Danilovgrad.

The rotund Crkva Sv Mučenika Stanka

TOP 10 OF EVERYTHING

Cathedral of the Resurrection of Christ, Podgorica

MUSEUMS

An elegantly furnished salon in King Nikola's Palace

1 Maritime Museum
🅿 B3 🏠 391 Trg Boheljske mornarice, Kotor 🕒 Hours vary, chech website 🌐 museummaritimum. com 🔗

Housed in the grand Baroque palace of the noble Grgurina family, this well-organized museum showcases the town's rich seafaring history and its role in Adriatic trade. Exhibits are spread across three floors and feature intricate model ships, sailors' uniforms, navigational tools, weapons and photographs, as well as a relief map of the bay.

2 Naval Heritage Collection
🅿 B3 🏠 Šetalište Porto Montenegro, Tivat 📞 067-637 781 🕒 9am–5pm Tue–Sat 🔗

A chance to clamber inside an authentic Yugoslav P821 submarine is the showpiece of this comprehensive naval museum. Across from the sub, the restored former arsenal building is an airy, light-filled space displaying over 300 artifacts including rare Austro-Hungarian naval machinery and the diaries of Montenegro's Princess Ksenija. The nautical-themed playground is an added attraction for families.

3 King Nikola's Palace
🅿 C3 🏠 4 Dvorshi Trg, Cetinje Crna Gora, Cetinje 🕒 Apr–Oct: 9am–5pm daily; Nov–Mar: 9am–3pm Mon–Fri 🌐 narodnimuzej.me/posjeta-muzej-kralja-nihole 🔗🅿

Originally, this 19th-century palace was built for King Nikola I, Montenegro's last monarch, but it was transformed into a museum after he was deposed in 1918. Despite suffering looting during World War II, enough of the original plush furnishings, family portraits and royal costumes remain to offer a peek into the opulence of royal life of the time. Entry is by guided tour only.

4 Museum of the Town
🅿 C4 🏠 11 Petra I Petrovića, Stari Grad, Budva 📞 033 453 308 🕒 8am–9pm Tue–Fri, 2–9pm Sat & Sun 🔗

Each floor of this historic townhouse museum is dedicated to a different era of Budva's colourful history, from prehistoric times to the modern era. There's an impressive display of Greek and Roman jewellery, as well as ceramics and glassware uncovered after the 1979 earthquake.

5 Museum of Local History
🅿 E6 🏠 Stari Grad bb, Ulcinj 📞 030-421 419 🕒 8am–8pm daily 🔗

Panoramic views over the Bay of Ulcinj are an added bonus at this Venetian-era palace. The museum offers a vivid portrayal of life from the 5th century BCE to the Ottoman period, with exhibits of traditional costumes, household objects and items recovered from shipwrecks.

6 Risan Mosaics Museum
🅿 B2 🏠 Gabela bb, Risan 🕒 8am–8pm Tue–Sun 🌐 muzejihotor.me/en/home/roman-mosaics 🔗🅿

Excavated in 1930, the foundations of this grand Roman villa revealed remarkably intact mosaic floors dating to the 2nd and 3rd centuries CE. The intricate

A mosaic of Hypnos, god of sleep, at the Risan Mosaics Museum

Montenegro's economic and numismatic history from ancient times to the euro. Exhibits include interactive displays of rare coins, banknotes and Montenegrin *perper*, the country's national currency before it became part of Yugoslavia.

patterned designs showcase the artistic skill of the Roman elite at the time.

7 Cat Museum

B3 Trg Gospa od Anđela - Stari Grad 371, Kotor 10am–6pm daily catsmuseum.org

Introduced to Kotor by early 20th-century sailors to solve the town's vermin problem, cats are considered a symbol of the town. Expect all sorts of feline-themed memorabilia, such as vintage artwork and jewellery in this whimsical museum. The entrance fee helps to care for the town's stray cats.

8 Money Museum

C3 Njegoševa 122, Cetinje Hours vary, chech website ccbcg. me/en/currency/money-museum

Set within the Central Bank building in Cetinje, the Money Museum recounts

9 House of Ivo Andrić

A3 Njegoševa 79, Herceg Novi 9am–9pm Mon–Sat, 10am–6pm Sun hnia.me

The former residence of Ivo Andrić celebrates the Nobel Prize-winning novelist, whose works focus on life under Ottoman rule in his native Bosnia. The museum preserves his literary legacy by displaying his personal belongings and manuscripts. Built in 1964 in Topla, the mansion served as his home after relocating to Herceg Novi from Belgrade with his wife, Milica.

10 City Museum

E3 Marha Miljanova 4, Podgorica 9am–8pm Tue–Sun pgmuzeji.me/en/muzej-grada

For a comprehensive overview of the capital's history and cultural heritage, head to the City Museum. Displays include everyday items, such as local folk costumes, weapons and coins, as well as pre-Christian bronzes and archaeological discoveries from the Roman town of Doclea, just outside the capital.

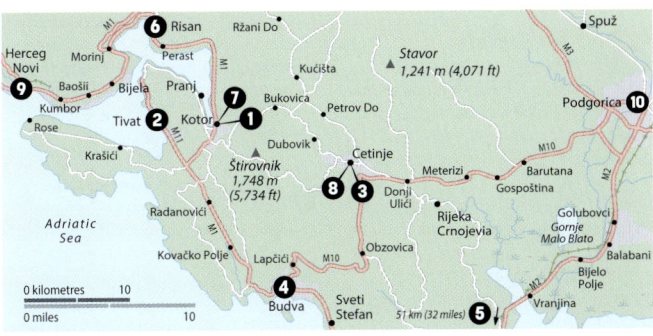

CHURCHES AND MONASTERIES

The large dome of the Cathedral of the Resurrection of Christ

1 Cathedral of the Resurrection of Christ

☉ E3 **⌂** 3 Bulevar Džordža Vašingtona, Podgorica **◷** Hours vary, chech website **ⓦ** hramvashrsenja.me

This striking cathedral may appear historic, but it's actually a modern addition to Podgorica's skyline, having only been consecrated in 2013. The design was inspired by Byzantine architecture, and combines historical and modern design elements, with a large dome and white stone towers topped with gold crosses. Inside, grand chandeliers illuminate gilded frescoes that cover nearly every inch of the cathedral.

2 Piva Monastery

This 16th-century Serbian Orthodox church (p114) was originally built by the Piva River during the Ottoman occupation, but was relocated in the late 1960s when the valley was flooded by the Mratinje Dam. Over the next 12 years, the entire premises – including a monk's house, bakery and enclosing walls – was moved to higher ground 8 km (5 miles) away. Fortunately, the frescoes, furnishings and ancient manuscripts all survived intact.

3 Ostrog Monastery

Carved into a dramatic cliff face, high above the Zeta Valley, this 17th-century monastery (p48) is the country's most important Orthodox Christian site. It is split into a Lower and Upper Monastery linked by a series of caves and narrow passageways. The Upper Monastery is impressive, but it's the Lower Monastery that is revered due to a belief its waters have healing powers.

4 Cathedral of St Tryphon

☉ B3 **⌂** Trg Sv Tripuna 336, Kotor **◷** 9am–6pm daily **ⓦ** kotorskabis kupija.me **⟳**

A striking mix of Romanesque and Gothic architecture, Kotor's Catholic cathedral is an impressive building. It was consecrated in 1166 but multiple earthquakes have necessitated many rebuilds, including in 1667 when the Baroque bell towers were added. Inside are several holy relics of St Tryphon himself, the patron saint of Kotor.

5 Church of St Nicholas

☉ B2 **⌂** Central Square, Perast **◷** 9am–5pm daily **ⓦ** stnicholas center.org

This 17th-century cathedral in the pretty town of Perast has never been completed. The original church was built in 1616, but attempts to expand it into a cathedral were abandoned during the Napoleonic Wars. Despite this, the site still features a soaring bell tower with three bronze bells and a Venetian clock. Climb to the top for panoramic views over the bay.

6 Our Lady of the Rocks

This small, blue-domed Catholic church (p84) atop an artificial island is shrouded in myths and legend. Supposedly, two fishers from Perast discovered an icon of the Virgin Mary on a rock in 1452 and vowed to build a

church in her honour. They created the island by dropping rocks into the bay, a tradition still practised every 22 July.

7 Church of the Holy Trinity

C4 Budva Old Town 068 711 076 Jun–Sep: 8am–10pm daily; Oct–May: 8am–noon, 4–7pm daily

After the fall of Venetian rule in Montenegro, the construction of a new church in the heart of Budva's Old Town was approved. The result is this 1804 Orthodox church with a distinctive façade of striped pink- and honey-coloured stone. The interior features beautiful frescoes and houses the tomb of local author Stefan Mitrov Ljubiša.

8 Savina Monastery

This complex (p86) outside of Herceg Novi might have the most beautiful setting in Montenegro, amid serene woodlands and overlooking the stunning coastline of the Adriatic Sea. The monastery is made of three churches, including one supposedly built by St Sava, the founder of the Serbian Orthodox Church. There is also a vineyard on-site with wine sold in the monastery's shop.

9 Morača Monastery

The Morača Monastery (p105) has occupied this site next to the Morača River since 1252, and is today a symbolic Orthodox site in Montenegro. The exteriors of the two churches may appear somewhat plain, but they mask an interior full of frescoes, including some by Serbian master painter Djordje Mitrofanović

10 St Luke's

B3 Trg Sv Luke, Kotor 9am–7pm Mon–Sat, 11am–7pm Sun

This compact 12th-century church has an unusual multi-faith history. Originally it was a Catholic church built in Romanesque and Gothic style, but following the Turkish War a second altar was built to serve an influx of Orthodox refugees. Though it was gifted to the Orthodox Church, it retains the two altars.

The verdant grounds of the Morača Monastery

TOWNS AND VILLAGES

maze of cobbled streets and secluded piazzas lined with palaces and churches. The architecture reflects centuries of Venetian influence as well as defensive precautions in case of Ottoman attack. The fortress walls above the town offer a steep but rewarding hike.

1 Bar
This lively student town and ferry port (p96) developed rapidly in the early 21st century. It now has a modern marina, wide boulevards and a renewed seafront lively with cafés, shops and restaurants. While it's popular among locals, it's often overlooked by tourists who make a beeline for the crumbling ruins of Stari Bar (p36), the stone fortress that sits in the rugged hills above Bar.

2 Perast
Wedged between the coast road and the Bay of Kotor, Perast (p44) is one of the Adriatic's most photogenic small towns. Historically it was a powerful Venetian port and key naval base, and these riches enabled it to construct elegant buildings, including 16 Baroque churches and 17 grand palazzos. Key landmarks include the 55-m (180-ft) bell tower of St Nicholas Church and the island church of Our Lady of the Rocks.

3 Kotor Old Town
With its dramatic fjord-like setting flanked by towering cliffs, Kotor's beautifully preserved Old Town (p32) is a UNESCO World Heritage Site. The medieval stone walls enclose a

4 Nikšić
Montenegro's second-biggest city (p103) is the country's industrial heart. It has a vibrant student population and is often referred to as the "beer capital" of Montenegro, thanks to its famous Nikšićko brewery. Founded by the Romans at the foot of Mount Trebjasa, the city is also home to several worth-while sights including the Royal Palace, Turkish castle and Church of St Basil.

5 Plav
Gateway to the Accursed Mountains and Prokletije National Park, Plav (p114) is a picturesque small town in northeast Montenegro. Set on the shores of Lake Plav, it's a haven for nature lovers who enjoy kayaking, hiking, fishing and soaking in the local hot springs. The town itself has Ottoman-era buildings, including the 16th-century Ali Pasha Mosque, and an Ethnographic Museum showcasing traditional local life.

6 Ulcinj
Close to the Albanian border, Ulcinj (p42) is known for its long sandy beaches, Ottoman-era Old Town and pirate history. The majority-Albanian population is evident in the numerous mosques, including the Pasha Mosque (213 CE) and the ruined sailors' mosque. The city beach, Mala Plaža (Small Beach), gets busy in summer, while south of town the 12-km (7-mile) Velika Plaža (Big Beach) is a hot spot for kitesurfers.

The village of Virpazar, on the shores of Lake Skadar

A clock tower in Herceg Novi's Old Town

7 Herceg Novi
Located at the entrance to the Bay of Kotor, Herceg Novi (p83) is known for its sunny climate and abundance of exotic plants brought by international sailors. Along the seafront are parks and gardens filled with palm trees, mimosas, oleanders and more, earning it the moniker "City of Flowers". Pretty, leaf-lined cobble-stone alleys and steps lead up to the Old Town Church of Archangel Michael and the Kanli Kula fortress.

8 Njeguši
The small mountain village Njeguši (p107) on the slopes of Mount Lovćen was the birthplace of the Petrović dynasty, which ruled Montenegro from the 17th to the 20th centuries. In the village, the ancestral home of King

Petar II Petrović-Njegoš has been preserved as a cultural museum. The area is also famed for its rustic regional cuisine, with local specialities including air-dried prosciutto, honey and smoked cheese.

9 Cetinje
High up in the Dinaric Alps, the former royal capital Cetinje (p46) is the spiritual and cultural heart of the country. The historic town hosts a number of grand palaces, elegant embassy buildings and museums that preserve the country's heritage, including the National Museum and the Museum of King Nikola. The Cetinje Monastery is the seat of Montenegro's Orthodox Church and an important pilgrimage site.

10 Virpazar
Virpazar (p98) is a traditional village on the shores of scenic Lake Skadar, with a few stone buildings, small restaurants and cafés scattered around its central square. It's the perfect gateway from which to explore Lake Skadar National Park (p26), a great place for boat tours, hiking, bird-watching and fishing. The village also sits within a key wine region and is renowned for its local Vranac wines and fresh fish dishes – be sure to linger here to try some.

NATURAL WONDERS

1 Tara River Canyon

Perhaps the most spectacular sight in Montenegro is this dramatic canyon (p113), which carves through the lofty mountains of Durmitor National Park (p22). It is the deepest canyon in Europe – reaching depths of 1,300-m (4,265-ft) – and the second-deepest in the world, following the Grand Canyon. The best way to experience its dramatic scenery is to go whitewater rafting along the Tara River or zip-lining beside the iconic Đurđevića Tara Bridge; both provide thrills and views aplenty.

2 Piva Canyon

This vast landmark canyon (p115) in northwest Montenegro was carved by the Piva River and features soaring cliffs up to 1,000 m (3,280 ft) high. In 1975, the area was flooded by the hydroelectric Mratinje Dam and the resulting Piva Reservoir is now a great spot for boating and kayaking. A scenic road clings to the cliffs of the canyon, offering a spectacular drive that passes through 56 tunnels.

3 Lake Skadar

Straddling Montenegro and Albania, Skadar (p26) is the largest lake in the Balkans. It's also the country's most famous birdlife reserve, with a wide variety of habitats and 280 bird species, including the rare Dalmatian pelican (p28). Yet birds aren't the only attraction here. This sprawling lake is also home to an array of traditional fishing villages, medieval monasteries and atmospheric fortress ruins. Boat tours around the lake set off from the welcoming gateway town of Virpazar (p98).

4 Nevidio Canyon

Formed during the last Ice Age, the impressive Nevidio Canyon (p116) is nearly 3 km (2 miles) long and up to 400 m (1,310 ft) deep. Some sections are extremely narrow and flanked by sheer cliffs, earning it the name Nevidio, which means "unseen" in Montenegrin. Guided canyoning excursions offer adrenaline-seekers the chance to navigate through the gorge by swimming, sliding, scrambling and jumping down numerous waterfalls and rapids.

The sloping hills and blue water of Piva Canyon

5 Blue Cave

Located on the Luštica Peninsula (p85) this incredible natural sea cave (p86) gets its name from the brilliantly illuminated blue water found inside. The grotto's unique lighting effects are created when sunlight reflects off the water, creating an iridescent glow. It's a popular spot for boat and kayaking tours but it's also possible to swim in the cave when it's not too busy and the water is calm.

6 Prokletije National Park

The last of Montenegro's five national parks (dedicated in 2009), the Prokletije Mountain range (p114) offers a quieter alternative to Durmitor's (p22) peaks. Its name translates to "Accursed Mountains", a name that matches the unforgiving landscapes here (all jagged peaks, glacial lakes and deep valleys, home to Balkan lynx, brown bear and chamois). It's one of the country's least explored areas but its challenging trails and epic views are worth the journey here.

7 Bobotov Kuk
⚓ K4

Bobotov Kuk is often regarded as the country's highest peak, standing proud at 2,523 m (8,278 ft) in Durmitor National Park (p22). The ascent is challenging and only suitable for experienced hikers (there are a few scrambling sections and part of the route also requiring cables), but you'll be rewarded with spectacular views, including of the Tara River Canyon. The trail passes through varied terrain, from alpine meadows to rocky ridges, and is a 6- to 8-hour round trip starting at the Sedlo Pass.

8 Biogradska Gora

One of Europe's last primeval forests, Biogradska Gora National Park (p113) spans 16 sq km (6 sq miles) of ancient forest, with towering beech, fir, juniper, white ash, maple and elm trees up to 500 years old. The park is also an incredibly biodiverse region, hosting some 2,000 plant species, 200 bird species and various mammals, including deer and bears. At its heart lies the glacial Biogradsko Lake, reached by scenic woodland trails.

9 Crno Jezero

Nestled at the foot of Mount Medjed in Durmitor National Park is the beautiful Black Lake (p113). It is actually two connected lakes, the Big Lake and Little Lake, both of which have clear waters ideal for swimming and kayaking. It can be reached by a pleasant 3-km (2-mile) walk from the nearby town of Žabljak (p116), and there's also a hiking trail around the lake's perimeter.

10 Lipa Cave

This extensive network of caves (p105) was only discovered in 1940, but is believed to have existed for millions of years. It's one of the country's largest cave systems with many tunnels and chambers filled with stalactites, stalagmites and natural pillars, as well as an underground river. The caves can only be explored by guided tour, which takes you to the cave from the car park via a train, and then deep underground.

The interior passageways of Lipa Cave

Clockwise from top
**The hulking
Piva Canyon; the
canyon's verdant
cliffs; rafting down
the Piva River**

BEACHES

1 Petrovac Beach
Set around a picturesque horseshoe bay beside the 16th-century Castle Lazaret, this sweep of sand (*p95*) is popular among families for its sheltered water and host of amenities. It's flanked by a seafront promenade, which promises a host of vibrant cafés and restaurants. If it's busy in summer, Lučice Beach (*p100*) around the headland is a quieter alternative.

2 Mogren
Accessed via a well-signposted coastal path just west of Budva's Old Town, Mogren (*p100*) is made up of two sandy beaches (Mogren I and Mogren II) connected by a short tunnel and wooden bridge. Both are backdropped by rocky cliffs and are beloved for their clear water, which is perfect for snorkelling. Facilities include a beach bar, changing room with showers, sun loungers and watersports rentals.

3 Sveti Stefan
With fine pale-pink pebbles, this beach (*p95*) is divided in two by a narrow causeway that leads to the eponymous 15th-century island village. While the northern end of the beach is usually reserved for guests of the luxurious Aman Sveti Stefan Hotel (temporarily closed), the southern end is free and ideal for swimming.

4 Velika Plaža
Appropriately named Big Beach (*p100*), Montenegro's longest beach, stretches for 12 km (7 miles) southeast of Ulcinj, towards the Albanian border. With vast empty swathes of golden sand and consistent winds, it's become one of Europe's top destinations for kitesurfing and windsurfing (there are several places to hire equipment). The water here is also surprisingly shallow, meaning it's possible to walk out for a while before you even get waist deep.

5 Pržno
A short drive from Budva, just off the coastal highway, Pržno Beach (*p95*) is a lovely stretch of pebble and

Picture-perfect Sveti Stefan, next to a scenic beach

8 Libera
🔲 E6

At the mouth of the Bojana River, right next to the Albanian border, is Ada Bojana (p100), an estuary island that formed after a ship ran aground here in the 19th century. Accessed via a bridge, the island's windswept beach Libera is popular with kitesurfers. At its northern end is a nudist resort.

9 Mala Plaza
🔲 E6

A 400-m (1,312-ft) crescent of soft golden sand framed by rocky cliffs, Ulcinj's main beach is an undeniably picturesque spot, and unsurprisingly the town's most popular. The seafront promenade buzzes with cafés, restaurants and ice-cream shops in summer while the historic Old Town, with its ancient stone buildings and small fortress, overlooks the beach from high up on a hill.

10 Murići

For a tranquil wild swim surrounded by nature, look no further than Murići (p100). Located on the southwest shore of Lake Skadar, this is the lake's only sandy beach. It's backed by the dramatic Rumija Mountains and accessed via a steep, winding road that descends from the surrounding highlands. The facilities are basic but it's a tranquil spot and the fresh water is warm and clear.

sand with clear, shallow waters and safe swimming zones. It's set against a backdrop of holiday villas, hotels and traditional stone buildings, and divided into a paid section with sun loungers and a free area for visitors.

6 Dobreč

On the west coast of the Luštica Peninsula, this small, secluded beach (p87) is hemmed in by thick forest and can only be reached by boat (it's a 30-minute water taxi-ride from the town of Herceg Novi). Measuring just 45 m (148 ft), the beautiful cove does get busy with day-trippers during the peak summer months – and with its exceptionally clear water and good restaurant, it's easy to see why.

7 Drobni Pijesak

A short detour off the coastal highway just north of Rijeka Reževići, this secluded little cove (p100) features a 240-m- (787-ft-) stretch of white pebbles and soft sand. There's no town or village in sight, just a small café tucked into the corner of the cove. The limited parking (and steep hike from the main road if you don't find a parking spot) keeps the crowds away, so you might have it all to yourself.

Murići beach, Lake Skadar's only sandy stretch

OUTDOOR ACTIVITIES

1 Hiking
With over two-thirds of the country covered in mountains, Montenegro offers abundant hiking opportunities. Durmitor National Park (p22) is a go-to for those looking for a challenge: it has a number of marked trails and peaks over 2,000 m (6,560 ft) that are accessible without the use of special equipment. Lovćen National Park (p40) is also a favourite, with scenic hikes promising sweeping views. Contact Montenegro's Mountaineering Association (pscg.me) to hire a guide if you'd rather not go it alone.

2 Skiing and Snowboarding
Less extensive, though considerably cheaper, than some of Europe's fashionable resorts, Montenegro has a decent ski infrastructure with reliable snow from January to March. The best-equipped resort is Kolašin (kolasin.me/kolasin-1450-ski-resort), in the Bjelasica mountains, but the slopes near Žabljak in Durmitor National Park (p22) are higher, catering to both beginners and serious skiers and snowboarders.

3 Kayaking
The sheltered waters within the Bay of Kotor and lily-covered Lake Skadar (p26) are both popular places for a paddle, with several operators offering tours, including Undiscovered Montenegro (undiscoveredmontenegro.com). Along the Adriatic coastline, sea kayakers can get up close to stunning karst cliffs, with excursions combining swimming and cliff-jumping.

4 Paragliding
Take to the skies to see the spectacular scenery from a different angle. Companies, including Paragliding Montenegro (paraglidingmontenegro.com), offer training courses or tandem flights for paragliding beginners. Want to glide over the Adriatic? Head to popular take-off spot Brajići, near Budva.

Skiing along the snowy peaks of Durmitor National Park

Prefer the peaks? Žabljak, in Durmitor National Park, is the gateway to epic mountain views.

5 Whitewater Rafting
The chance to raft through the world's second-largest canyon (the Tara River; p113) is a major draw for adventure enthusiasts. This popular route features grade II to IV rapids and passes under the spectacular Tara Bridge (p116). Those looking for a more gentle ride should make a beeline for the Morača River and Lim River instead.

6 Swimming
The Adriatic's beautiful beaches, coves and islands provide ample opportunities for swimming. Kotor Bay has calm, sheltered waters and a dramatic fjord backdrop, while the pebble beaches near Budva (p30) and the sandy shores of Ulcinj (p42) are great spots for a dip. For a freshwater alternative, try Lake Skadar (p26).

7 Bird-watching
Sitting on the Adriatic Flyway, an important migratory route between Europe and Africa, Montenegro hosts over 350 bird species. Key sites include

Lake Skadar *(p26)* for waterfowl such as the rare Dalmatian pelican, Durmitor National Park *(p22)* for the black woodpecker and the forest of Biogradska Gora *(p113)* for species like the European honey buzzard.

8 Canyoning

A combination of climbing, sliding, jumping and swimming through gorges and waterfalls, canyoning is an adventurous way to explore the country's wild landscape. Popular spots include the dramatic Nevidio *(p116)* near Durmitor, Sopot near Herceg Novi *(p83)* and Rikavac near Bar *(p96)*; the latter is suitable for kids.

9 Scuba Diving

Colourful fish aren't the only things you'll spot when diving in Montenegro. The Adriatic coast is dotted with more unusual underwater features, such as caves, submarine tunnels and shipwrecks dating to World War II, all of which can be seen on guided excursions. Sign up at dive schools in Budva, Przno and Ulcinj from June to October (when the water is warm and visibility at its best).

10 Kitesurfing

Thanks to its reliable wind and calm water, Montenegro has become one of Europe's top kitesurfing spots. The best-known location is Velika Plaža (Big Beach), near Ulcinj *(p42)*, which stretches for 12 km (7 miles) along the Adriatic coast. Nearby, Ada Bojana is also a popular hub, with kite schools offering equipment hire and tuition for all skill levels.

Kitesurfing in the calm waters off Montenegro's coast

TOP 10
HIKING TRAILS

1. Peaks of the Balkans Trail
The hike of hikes, this epic 92-km (57-mile) signposted trail weaves through the remote and unspoiled mountain regions of Montenegro, Albania and Kosovo.

2. Subra
A scenic six-hour sea-to-summit hike from Herceg Novi to the top of Subra mountain (1,680 m/5,510 ft).

3. Bobotov Kuk
From the Sedlo Pass, it's a challenging 9.8-km (6-mile) return hike to scale Montenegro's mythic peak, located in Durmitor National Park. The route includes ferrata-style ropes and cables, and is best reserved for experienced hikers.

4. Razvršje
This scenic trail leads from Biogradsko Lake through dense forest to the summit of Razvršje (2,033 m/6,670 ft).

5. Kom Kucki
Conquering the highest peak in Komovi (Montenegro's eastern mountain range) takes around three hours, with a steep scramble to reach the summit at 2,487 m (8,160 ft).

6. Vrmac Massif
This relatively flat 5.5-km (3.5-mile) ridge walk offers panoramic views over the beautiful Bay of Kotor.

7. Karanfili
It's a steep but spectacular climb to summit this three-headed mountain, ascending 1,400 m (4,590 ft) in 6.6 km (4 miles) on the border of Albania.

8. Black Lake
This leisurely loop through ancient pine forests circumnavigates the lake and takes around 80 minutes; it's a great pick for families.

9. Maglic
The trail from Montenegro to Bosnia and Herzegovina's highest peak promises unforgettable scenery.

10. Durmitor Circuit
This multi-day circular route winds through dramatic landscapes of high peaks, lush valleys and glacial lakes.

WILDLIFE

1 Nose-horned Viper
One of the few venomous species native to Montenegro, this thin snake gets its name from the horn-like protuberance on its nose. Preferring rocky outcrops, scrubland and forest edges, it can be found in the mountains of Prokletije *(p114)* and Durmitor *(p22)*, as well as coastal regions near Herceg Novi *(p83)* and Kotor *(p32)*. While generally shy, it can be aggressive when threatened (and it's best to keep your distance if you spot one).

2 Grey Wolf
Montenegro is home to a few hundred wolves, found mainly in the northern regions of Prokletije *(p114)* and Biogradska Gora *(p113)* – though they also thrive in various forests, mountains and grasslands around the country. Wolves are social creatures, typically living and hunting in packs of up to ten, and preying on herbivores including deer, wild boar and sheep.

3 Balkan Lynx
This critically endangered subspecies of the Eurasian lynx is native to the remote mountains of Prokletije National Park *(p114)*. Like most cats, they're nocturnal hunters, preying on small mammals such as rabbits and roe deer. Their distinctive tufted ears and

The distinctive nose-horned viper, a snake best avoided

dark spotted coat help them camouflage in their forest habitat. And with fewer than 50 individuals left in the wild, you'd be very lucky to see one.

4 Eurasian Brown Bear
Weighing up to 400 kg (880 lbs) and standing 2 m (7 ft) tall on their hind legs, brown bears are Montenegro's largest mammal. These powerful omnivores are apex predators, playing a vital role in the local ecosystem and primarily inhabiting the dense mountain forests of Durmitor *(p22)* and Biogradska Gora *(p113)* national parks. Just over 120 of them remain in the country, making them a protected species.

5 European Wildcat
The European wildcat is a solitary feline found in Montenegro's shady forests (places like Biogradska Gora and Lovćen national parks promise sighting opportunities). Though similar in appearance to domestic cats, they are more robust and have a bushier tail. They are also adaptable to various habitats and play a crucial role in controlling populations of rodents such as voles, mice and rats. However,

A Balkan lynx, found in Montenegro's alpine forests

the wildcat faces threats from habitat loss in developing areas of Montenegro and hybridization with domestic cats.

6 Griffon Vulture

These large birds, also known as the Eurasian griffon, operate as scavengers in the rugged areas around Lake Skadar (p26) and the Prokletije Mountains (p114), where they seek out safe nesting sites on cliffs and rocky ledges. With a wingspan of up to 3 m (9 ft), they're easy to spot and can often be seen in flocks over open areas, using thermal updrafts to conserve energy while searching for carcasses.

7 Dalmatian Pelican

Lake Skadar (p26) is home to the Dalmatian pelican, one of the largest and most recognizable birds in the region, thanks to their impressive wingspan of up to 3.6 m (12 ft) and distinctive long, curved bill, which they use to scoop up fish from the water. They rely on wetland habitats and can often be seen gliding over the lake.

8 Hermann's tortoise

Known for its distinctive patterned shell, this small terrestrial tortoise can reach up to 25 cm (1 ft) in length. They are native to Montenegro and prefer dry, sunny habitats such as Mediterranean scrub and low-density woodlands, which can be found along the coastal region and in Lovćen National Park (p40). Due to habitat destruction and illegal collection they are now a protected species.

9 Balkan Chamois

The Balkan chamois is a mountain goat-antelope found in the high-altitude regions of Montenegro. Growing up to 80 cm (2.5 ft) tall, they are agile and well adapted to steep terrain, often seen climbing rocky outcrops. Their main predators include wolves and eagles, but they are also still hunted by humans for their meat and leather.

10 Golden Eagle

This powerful bird of prey, known for its striking golden plumage, is a common sight in the mountains of Montenegro, where it soars effortlessly through the skies. Their keen eyesight makes them skilled hunters, primarily feeding on small- to medium-sized mammals and birds. Durmitor National Park (p22) is a particularly good area to see them.

The golden eagle, a bird of prey common in Montenegro

VIEWPOINTS

1 Đurđevića Tara Bridge
The Đurđevića Tara Bridge *(p116)* offers dizzying views of Europe's deepest canyon and the turquoise Tara River below. Completed in 1940, the bridge is an engineering marvel with five elegant arches, spanning 365 m (1,198 ft) and connecting the two sides of the canyon. Travellers can park at either end of the bridge and walk across. Better yet, take in the views from the high-speed zip line nearby *(p118)*.

2 Sveti Stefan
This tiny fortified island village *(p95)* is one of Montenegro's most photogenic sights. Its cluster of 15th-century stone villas is accessed via a causeway, flanked by pink-sand beaches and lapped by the azure Adriatic Sea. The whole island is privately owned by a luxury hotel, meaning it's off limits to the public, but there are excellent elevated views from the nearby coastal road and St Sava Church.

3 Njegoš Mausoleum
The star attraction in Lovćen National Park *(p40)* is this site found at the top of its second-highest peak, Jezerski Vrh. From the car park to the mausoleum it's a breath-stealing 461 steps, but once you reach the circular observation platform you're rewarded with epic views of the rugged peaks across the Bay of Kotor and Adriatic coast. Access to the viewing platform is free and can be visited even when the mausoleum is closed.

4 Kotor Serpentine
📍 C3
The winding road from Kotor to Lovćen offers dramatic views over the Bay of Kotor, but it's no easy drive. Steep and narrow, the route features no less than 25 hairpin turns and requires cautious driving. Fortunately, there are several lay-bys where drivers can safely pull over to take a photograph of the sweeping panorama.

5 The Spanish Fortress
📍 A3
From its hilltop perch, Herceg Novi's Spanish Fortress offers commanding views over the Bay of Kotor and the Adriatic Sea, sometimes as far as the Croatian coast if the sky is clear. It's a particularly atmospheric spot at sunset, with the pretty town's terracotta-roofed houses clustered on the hillside below. To get there, follow signposts from the main road then take an unmarked left turn just past Srbina 34.

The soaring Đurđevića Tara Bridge, which crosses the Tara River Canyon

6 Ostrog Monastery

Carved into a vertical cliff face, Ostrog (p48) sits high above the surrounding landscape at a height of 900 m (2,952 ft). Its elevated position adds to the serene, spiritual atmosphere, with breathtaking drops below and 180-degree views over the distant plains. The approach road is narrow and steep, ending at a parking area near the Lower Monastery. From here, you can walk or take a shuttle to the Upper Monastery.

7 Kotor Fortress Walls

B3 **May–Sep 8am–8pm daily**

Kotor's (p32) historic town walls rise steeply above the Old Town to Kotor Fortress (St John's Fortress). While it's a steep, challenging climb of 1,350 steps, the views over the Old Town's rooftops, with the Bay of Kotor beyond, make it well worth the effort. The main entrances are signposted from the River Gate and North Gate.

8 Pavlona Strana (Rijeka Crnojevića)

D3

Want to snap that famous postcard picture of Lake Skadar National Park (p26)? Take the winding P16 road from

The meandering Rijeka Crnojevića River, near Lake Skadar

Podgorica to Virpazar, stopping in the lay-by near the horseshoe bend of the Rijeka Crnojevića River (it's at the northwest end of the lake). The viewpoint here offers great views of the river as it curves elegantly around a steeply forested hill towards the iconic lake.

9 Our Lady of the Rocks

One of two small islands in the Bay of Kotor, Our Lady of the Rocks (p84) is located 500 m (1,640 ft) offshore from the town of Perast (p44). It's a stunning sight, its striking blue-domed, 17th-century church set against the backdrop of spectacular mountains. Visitors can view it fine enough from Perast's lovely waterfront, but it's even better close up – boats run regularly from the harbour, taking 10 to 15 minutes.

10 Piva Canyon

Picture a bright blue river winding its way through a lush green landscape. That's the Piva Canyon, and it's just as incredible as it sounds. Located north of Plužine, this dramatic canyon (p114) was carved by the Piva River thousands of years ago, reaching depths of up to 1,000 m (3,280 ft) and stretching for 50 km (30 miles). The best views are from the Mratinje Dam or the sinuous M18 road, which passes through 56 tunnels as it clings to the steep mountainside.

FAMILY ATTRACTIONS

1 Take to the Skies
For incredible views of Kotor Bay, hop on Kotor's thrilling cable car *(p88)*. It takes just 11 minutes to ascend to Kuk village where an array of family-friendly activities await: there's a fortress to explore, playgrounds and a short alpine rollercoaster *(p40)*. If you feel the need for more speed, why not fly across the Tara River Canyon *(p113)* by zip line? Reaching speeds of up to 120 km/h (75 mph), the 90-second "extreme" ride offers an unforgettable rush. There are two shorter lines available, too, so children as young as three can fly in tandem with a guide.

2 Family-friendly Beaches
The Adriatic coast offers several sheltered swimming spots, often with marked safe zones and a lifeguard on duty. Family favourites include Jaz Beach near Budva, with its shallow water and soft sand, Petrovac Beach for its gentle waves, and Plavi Horizonti in the Bay of Tivat. Lake Skadar *(p26)* and Crno Jezero (Black Lake; *p113*) are accessible freshwater options.

3 Ice Cream on the Coast
Montenegro's Italian-style *gelaterias* are the stuff childhood dreams are made of, with dozens of mouth-watering flavours from classic chocolate and vanilla to local ingredients such as fig, walnut and honey (reflecting the country's cultural heritage). Moritz Eis *(moritzeis.com)* is a popular brand of artisanal gelato with parlours found all along the coast, while Marshall's *(marshallsgelato.com)* in Kotor Old Town is a perennial favourite.

4 Fascinating Museums
When rainy days force the family indoors, Montenegro's museums *(p52)* are here to help. For those interested in the sea, there are plenty of options: make waves at the nautical-themed

Enjoying the views from Kotor's scenic cable car

playground in Tivat's Naval Heritage Collection *(p52)* or gaze at model ships in Kotor's Maritime Museum *(p52)*. There's also the quirky Cat Museum *(p53)* in Kotor, which is packed with feline-themed exhibits bound to entertain the kids.

5 Curious Caves
Montenegro's karst landscape is riddled with caves, but none more impressive than Lipa Cave *(p105)*. This underground world of dark passageways and caverns is filled with ancient stalactites and stalagmites. Guides lead the way, sharing interesting stories and facts about how the cave was formed and the wildlife that inhabits it. With a constant temperature of 8–12°C, it's also a good place to escape the summer heat. Those looking for somewhere a little less spooky can explore the Blue Cave *(p86)* – boat tours here allow visitors to swim in the iridescent blue water beneath the rocks.

6 Lake Skadar
With its serene setting and calm, lily-covered water, Lake Skadar *(p26)* is perfect for family adventures. Quiet beaches provide places to relax while the gentle water is great for paddling. Most kayaking tours start from the

fishing village of Virpazar (p98), where you can visit the ruined island fortress of Ostrvo Grmožur and stop for a dip on secluded beaches like Mali and Veliki Šdrič.

7 Easy Hikes

Stretching up the mountainside behind Kotor's Old Town, the hike up Kotor Fortress (p69) is a good challenge for little legs. The path is steep but well maintained, following medieval stone walls. Counting the steps is a good distraction (though you probably won't remember all 1,350) but be sure to set off early and factor in plenty of rest stops. The scenic loop around Crno Jezero (p113), in Durmitor National Park, is another easy hike.

8 On the Water

Montenegro's top rafting destination is the turquoise Tara River, which flows through the world's second-deepest canyon. Along with dramatic scenery, the river has a mix of gentle and adventurous rapids, suitable for ages three and above. Tours are led by experienced guides and include stop-offs for swimming, rock-jumping and visits to nearby waterfalls. The Morača and Liman rivers are more sedate, especially in summer when water levels are low.

9 Old Town Wanderings

While grown-ups marvel at the incredibly well-preserved medieval and Venetian architecture in Montenegro's old towns, kids will feel like they've stepped back in time in these historic centres. Seek out atmospheric places like Kotor, Budva, Perast and Herceg Novi for urban adventures.

10 Bird-watching

Montenegro may be rife with wildlife (p66), but much of it is suitably wild and often impossible to glimpse. Eurasian brown bears and Balkan lynx prowl the remote mountains, while European wildcats hide in the forests. Montenegro's birdlife, however, is much more accessible. Families can spot griffon vultures and Dalmatian pelicans on Lake Skadar, while golden eagles can be seen around Durmitor (p22).

Rafting on the crystal-clear Tara River

LOCAL DISHES

1 Pršut
This traditional Montenegrin dry-cured ham, renowned for its rich flavour and distinct aroma, is perhaps the country's most famous export. Hailing from the village of Njeguši (*p107*), on the slopes of Mount Lovćen, it's made from high-quality pork and undergoes a long process of salting, seasoning and air-drying before it's ready to eat. Try it with fresh bread or as part of a classic Montenegrin platter of cheese, olives, grapes and figs.

2 Montenegrin Lamb
Lamb in milk is a firm favourite at family gatherings, particularly in the highlands of northern Montenegro. Traditionally cooked in a bell-shaped pot over low coals, the meat is slowly braised in milk with root vegetables (such as carrots and parsnips), rose-mary, parsley and garlic. The result is delicate, tender and full of flavour.

3 Kačamak
A comfort food staple made from cornmeal (and sometimes crushed potatoes and cheese), *kačamak* resembles a thick polenta. It developed in the 18th century as the impoverished country was struggling to survive against the threat of Ottoman invasion, and it's still served today (particularly in rural restaurants around Kolasin and Durmitor National Park). Pair it with a hearty meat stew and you've got the perfect fuel for a day in the mountains.

Flaky *burek*, a popular pastry in Montenegro

4 Ćevapčići
Montenegro's staple street food, these small sausage patties are made from a blend of minced beef, lamb or pork, seasoned with spices and herbs. They can be skewered and grilled with onions or peppers, or served with a chunky tomato and cucumber salad, a healthy dollop of creamy *kajmak* (similar to clotted cream) and warm Mediterranean flatbread.

5 Black Risotto
Montenegro offers seafood in abundance, but locals will tell you that this fish-infused risotto is a highlight. Best enjoyed at a seaside café in the Bay of Kotor, the dish is flavoured with garlic, onions and white wine before bits of squid and shellfish are added, followed by a sprinkle of parsley. But what makes it so special? Due to the added squid or cuttlefish ink, the rice appears a striking black colour.

6 Burek
Found at pretty much every bakery in Montenegro, these Balkan pastries are deliciously moreish. The flaky filo dough is typically stuffed with mincemeat, cheese, mushrooms, spinach or potatoes, usually served hot and sometimes accompanied by yoghurt and a side salad. They aren't just savoury, however. Sweet fillings, such as apples or cherries, make for a tasty breakfast.

7 Njeguski Sir
Originating from the Njeguši region, this semi-hard cheese is made from sheep or cow's milk and is known for its rich, creamy texture. It has a distinctive flavour, which ranges from mild to sharp depending on how long it's aged. Traditionally the cheese is lightly smoked and enjoyed as part of a charcuterie board, pairing beautifully with cured meats, olives and a glass of local wine.

Freshly caught local carp on the waters of Lake Skadar

8 Lake Skadar Carp

How do you like your carp? A prized delicacy in Montenegro, Lake Skadar carp can be prepared in various ways. Some locals roast it with dried fruits while others smoke the fish over a fire then marinate it in oil and herbs. Another popular preparation is carp in salt, where the fish is coated in salt and herbs before baking, enhancing its natural flavours. Carp stew, where the fish is cooked with vegetables, spices and wine, is also a go-to.

9 Buzara

Showcasing the region's rich maritime flavours, this traditional seafood dish is popular on the Adriatic coast. It's made using shellfish, such as mussels, shrimp or clams, and cooked in a simple yet flavourful sauce of olive oil, garlic, white wine and parsley. Buzara is best served with a side helping of crusty bread, which can be used to soak up the delicious sauce.

10 Palacinke

Similar to crêpes, these pancakes have a delicate texture and can be enjoyed sweet or savoury. Delicious fillings include jam, banana or nuts, but they can also be dusted with powdered sugar or drizzled with honey. Eurocrem – a local spread made from hazelnut, cocoa and milk – is also a Montenegro favourite. Prefer your pancakes savoury? Try the *palacinke* packed with ham, cheese and spinach.

TOP 10
LOCAL DRINKS

1. Rakija
A strong fruit brandy, often made from plums or grapes, enjoyed as a traditional aperitif.

2. Vranac
A rich, red wine native to Montenegro, known for its bold flavour and deep aroma.

3. Krstač
A local white wine made from a unique grape variety. Crisp and aromatic, it's perfect for summer.

4. Montenegrin Beer
Local breweries produce various beers, with refreshing Nikšićko being the most popular.

5. Macedonian Wine
This sweet, fruity wine, often enjoyed with meals, is a highlight from Montenegro's vineyards.

6. Homemade Juice
Freshly squeezed juices from local fruits like oranges, pomegranates and figs are incredibly refreshing.

7. Medovina
This sweet honey wine is made by fermenting honey and water and often enjoyed chilled.

8. Fruit Liqueurs
Locally crafted liqueurs made from various fruits make for a sweet and flavourful drink.

9. Kafa
Traditional Montenegrin coffee is typically served strong and unfiltered, but it can be toned down with milk.

10. Tamarind Drink
A refreshing beverage made from tamarind fruit, known for its sweet and tangy flavour.

A line-up of refreshing homemade juices

NIGHTS OUT

Revellers enjoying a DJ set on the beach in Montenegro

1 Beach Clubs

Looking to party on the coast? Head to one of Montenegro's scenic beach clubs. A chic alternative to city nightlife, these sophisticated venues offer days filled with luxurious beach-side pampering followed by evenings of sunset cocktails and DJ sets. Popular venues include Almara Beach Club *(067 105 898)* in Luštica Bay, Dukley Beach Lounge *(dukleyhotels.com)* in Budva and Buddha-Bar Beach *(buddhabar. com/en/beachclubs/montenegro)* in Porto Montenegro.

2 Evening Strolls

Once the beachgoers have gone home and the heat of the day has subsided, Montenegro's seafront promenades are lovely places for an evening stroll. In towns like Budva, Kotor and Tivat, these promenades are lined with high-end bars and restaurants, where visitors can dine al fresco, listen to live music and soak up the atmosphere, all while being cooled by a gentle sea breeze.

3 Sunset Boat Trips

If sailing towards the sunset, glass of local wine in hand, sounds like the perfect way to end your day, book a boat trip. Montenegro J Sailing *(montenegrojsailing.me)* offers four-hour private charters from Kotor towards the picturesque town of Perast, with traditional Montenegrin drinks and nibbles on board. Numerous operators in Herceg Novi and Tivat also provide scenic sunset cruises; head to the waterfront to enquire about options.

4 Traditional Taverns

A cornerstone of Montenegrin social life, *kafanas* are traditional Balkan tavernas that serve *rakija (p73)*, local wines and hearty dishes, frequently accompanied by live folk bands. They're a great place to cosy up if you're looking for a more chilled, and typically Montenegrin, evening. Kafana Porto, in the rural village of Njeguši *(p107)*, is a favourite.

5 Theatre Nights

Culture-lovers will find plenty of action in Montenegro's towns and cities, with performances throughout the year. The Montenegrin National Theatre *(cnp.me)* in Podgorica is the

Sunset over the Bay of Kotor, a scenic spot for a boat trip

Top Hill Club, a huge outdoor venue in Budva

country's leading venue, with classic and contemporary plays, often featuring local talent. For more intimate drama and dance acts, see what's on at Kotor's Nikola Djurkovic Cultural Centre *(kckotor.me)* or in the open-air amphitheatre in Herceg Novi's *(p83)* Kanli Kula fortress.

6 Wine Bars
With its long history of viticulture, Montenegro isn't lacking in top-notch wineries. Crush Wine Station *(067 260 614)* in Porto Montenegro has an extensive list of local vintages, with terrific views of Tivat Marina to boot. For something a little different, book a table at Kraken Floating Winebar *(underwaterwine.me)* where you can sample wines that have been aged at the bottom of the sea. Keen swimmers can go for a dip before starting their tastings, too.

7 Jazz Clubs
Montenegrins love their jazz and clubs dedicated to the genre are always buzzing. Two of the country's most famous include Podgorica's Ethno Jazz Club *(sejdefa.com)*, which promises Mediterranean-style jazz, and Jazz Club Evergreen *(p90)*, which hosts regular live international and local acts in Kotor's Old Town. To keep your finger on the pulse about local events, tune into JazzMNE *(jazzmne.com)*, a Montenegrin radio station dedicated to the genre.

8 Live Music
Thanks to its Mediterranean climate, many of the country's best live music venues are in historical open-air settings. Bedem Fortress near Nikšić and Kanli Kula Fortress in Herceg Novi have seasonal programmes, while Jaz Beach near Budva and Velika Plaža *(p100)* in Ulcinj both host popular music festivals. Podgorica's CKZ Ribnica *(067 200 575)* cultural centre also has regular live performances, from traditional Balkan tunes to jazz and rock.

9 LGBTQ+ scene
LGBTQ+ nightlife in Montenegro is gradually evolving, particularly in urban areas like Podgorica and Budva. Budva's beach clubs and bars, such as Top Hill *(tophill.me)*, offer welcoming spaces for the LGBTQ+ community, while Casper Bar *(033 402 290)* in the Old Town is an unofficial LGBTQ+ hangout for coffee by day and cocktails by night. Kotor's Old Town also has several gay-friendly bars and clubs.

10 Cool Clubs
Montenegro's late-night circuit tends to be focused in coastal holiday spots, with Budva considered the party capital. Super-clubs include Budva's open-air Top Hill, with a capacity for 5,000 people, and Maximus *(067 217 101)* in Kotor's Old Town, which features multilevel dance floors and a stage for live music. Both have a thrilling summer line-up with world-class DJs.

FESTIVALS AND EVENTS

1 Carnival
Feb
Rooted in Venetian Renaissance tradition, the centuries-old winter carnival is a major event in Kotor. The whole town is turned into a performance venue for the near month-long festivities – the elaborate floats and costumes donned by carnival groups are must-sees.

2 Mimosa Festival
Feb/Mar
The blooming of yellow mimosa flowers – which symbolize renewal in the local culture – heralds the beginning of spring in Herceg Novi. To celebrate, the town puts on a host of events, starting with a parade of brass bands and majorettes. Live music, flower exhibitions and traditional costume shows follow.

3 Lim Regatta
Last weekend in May
For three days every year, watersports enthusiasts from across the region gather to take part in this adrenaline-fuelled rafting event. Participants navigate 134 km (83 miles) of the River Lim, all the way from its source at Lake Plav to the confluence of the River Lim and River Milesevka at Prijepolje, Serbia. The route takes about 20 hours to complete.

4 Fasinada
22 July
Every year on 22 July, the coastal town of Perast commemorates the discovery of a religious icon at Our Lady of the Rocks (p84) in 1452. Locals form a convoy of fishing boats and throw rocks into the sea beside the church, re-creating how the island was formed.

5 Blueberry Festival
July/August
Held in Plav (p114) each summer, this two-week festival is dedicated to the region's abundant wild blueberries. Events showcase the town's agricultural heritage with blueberry-picking contests, parades and tasting sessions of jams, juices and rajika (p73). The festival culminates with the crowning of "Miss Blueberry" on the final day.

6 Herceg Novi-Montenegro Film Festival
Aug ⓦ filmfestival.me
One of Montenegro's most important cultural events, this annual celebration of cinema from southeastern Europe features a diverse line-up of regional and international films, screened in spectacular open-air venues.

7 Boka Nights
3 Aug
Though it can be traced back to 18th-century celebrations in Venice, Boka Nights is today a grand celebration of Kotor's maritime heritage. At its heart is a huge parade of decorated boats, which set off from the village of Muo and journey to Dobrata and back,

A performer at Kotor's extravagant winter Carnival

finishing with fireworks. The party continues in the Old Town *(p32)* with music and dancing into the early hours.

8 Perast Klapa Festival
Sep w festivalklapaperast.com

Meaning "group of friends", *klapa* is a UNESCO-recognized form of traditional acapella characterized by harmonious tunes. The style originated on the Dalmatian coast and this festival seeks to preserve it through gathering groups from Montenegro and Croatia to perform in front of the stunning Church of St Nicholas in Perast *(p44)*.

9 Petrovac Jazz Festival
Sep w petrovacjazzfestival.webnode.page

This multiday jazz extravaganza brings together renowned international musicians and emerging artists for a celebration of all things jazz. Performances often take place in open-air venues, set against the backdrop of the Adriatic Sea.

10 Wine and Bleak Festival
Dec

The lakeside town of Virpazar *(p98)* is best known for two things: local wine and the lake fish called bleak. This winter festival celebrates both with wine competitions and tasting sessions, fishing demonstrations and folk music.

TOP 10 TRADITIONAL HOLIDAYS

1. Orthodox Christmas
6–7 Jan
A religious holiday marking the birth of Jesus; locals attend church services, prepare feasts and light yule logs.

2. International Women's Day
8 Mar
A public holiday celebrating the social, economic, cultural and political achievements of the nation's women.

3. Easter
Mar/Apr
A country-wide celebration with religious services, egg painting and festive meals such as roast lamb.

4. Labour Day
1 May
Workers are celebrated with outdoor activities and gatherings.

5. Victory Day
9 May
Military parades and ceremonies commemorate the country's victory over fascism during World War II.

6. Independence Day
21 May
Parades, flag-raising ceremonies and festivities honour the day Montenegro gained independence from Serbia.

7. National Day
13 July
Marks the country's recognition as an independent nation in 1878, and the anti-fascist rebellion of 1941.

8. All Saints' Day
1 Nov
Catholics visit cemeteries, light candles and honour their deceased loved ones with prayers and blessings.

9. Njegoš Day
13 Nov
National hero Petar II Petrović-Njegoš is celebrated with cultural events, poetry readings and wreath-laying.

10. New Year's Eve
31 Dec
Family gatherings, fireworks and festivities welcome the new year.

MONTENEGRO FOR FREE

1 Bird-Watching
There's no cost to looking up at the skies. Montenegro is a popular bird-watching destination, and for good reason. Its varied habitats and compact size means that a short drive can take you from coastal saltpans to primeval mountain forests, allowing bird-watchers the opportunity to spot a host of species in just a few hours.

2 Beautiful Beaches
With an Adriatic coastline stretching over 280 km (174 miles), Montenegro isn't short of beautiful beaches. While some stretches are owned by beach clubs or luxury hotels, most are publicly accessible without the need to pay for sunloungers or umbrellas. Budva's (p30) Jaz and Mogren beaches have safe swimming areas, while the Luštica Peninsula (p85) offers quieter spots.

3 Scenic Hikes
Hiking is one of the best ways to immerse yourself in Montenegro's natural beauty and it needn't cost you a penny. There's an excellent network of hiking trails (p65) around the country, with free parking in more remote areas. While the five national parks offer the most spectacular trails, note that they do have a small entry fee.

4 Free Festivals
From winter carnivals to wine festivities, boat races to blueberry harvests, Montenegro's array of local events (p76) offers cultural immersion at its most thrilling. During the summer months, free outdoor concerts, art exhibitions and traditional folklore shows are also common around the country.

5 Promenade Walks
Montenegro's beaches might be the main draw along the coast, but the country's waterfront promenades are equally scenic. Tivat's (p84) Porto Montenegro features a luxurious marina with a paved waterfront path, while the Budva Riviera (p94) offers miles of scenic coastline, perfect for leisurely walks. Kotor's waterfront promenade along the Bay of Kotor is also free to explore, providing breathtaking views of the surrounding mountains and sea.

6 Churches and Monasteries
Most of Montenegro's religious buildings offer free entry to visitors. Ostrog Monastery (p48), dramatically positioned on a cliff edge, is a must-see pilgrimage site. Other impressive free-to-visit places include the 13th-century Morača Monastery (p105) and the elegant Savina Monastery (p86); the latter offers great views of the Bay of Kotor.

7 Historical Sites
Explore the ruins of Stari Bar (p36), soak up the views from Kotor's fortress (p69), step back in time in Ulcinj's cobblestone lanes (p42):

Walking along a coastal promenade in the Bay of Kotor

Montenegro's historical sites are just as spectacular as its natural landscapes – and many are free to explore.

8 Parks and Gardens

Montenegro's parks and gardens provide serene spaces to take a break from sightseeing or enjoy a shady picnic away from the heat of the day. Podgorica (p104) has a number of green spaces, including the King's Park which features sculptures along the riverside. The 19th-century gardens around Cetinje's (p46) Royal Palace also make for a romantic retreat.

9 Museums

While some museums (p52) in Montenegro charge a small fee, many offer free entry on special days or have free sections. The Money Museum (p53) in Cetinje recounts the history of the country's currency and is free to enter. Meanwhile, smaller local museums in towns like Cetinje (p46) offer free admission at certain times.

10 Open-air Markets

Make a beeline for Montenegro's outdoor markets for affordable, local produce and souvenirs. Buzzy Kotor Market, near the Old Town (p32), and Podgorica's Gintaš farmers' market are local favourites.

A traditional Montenegrin plate, sold in Kotor Market

TOP 10
BUDGET TIPS

Products on display in a local store in Kotor

1. Take the Bus
Montenegro's extensive bus network is a reliable and affordable way to travel between cities and towns.

2. Dine at Local Konobas
Konobas (traditional taverns) serve delicious homemade dishes at lower prices than tourist restaurants.

3. Stay in Guesthouses
Family-run guesthouses have comfortable rooms at a fraction of the cost of hotels.

4. Take Advantage of Off-Peak Travel
Travel during the shoulder seasons (April–June and September–October) to find better deals on flights, accommodation and attractions.

5. Free Tours
Companies such as Montenegro Hostel *(montenegrohostel.com)* run free walking tours in Budva, Kotor and Podgorica.

6. Pay in Cash
Pay in euros to avoid foreign transaction fees.

7. Look for Happy Hour
Many bars and clubs have happy hour deals, especially in Budva and Kotor.

8. Explore Small Towns
Smaller towns, like Perast or Herceg Novi, usually offer lower prices on food and accommodation.

9. Get Some Local Insight
Don't be afraid to ask Montenegrins for advice, they're unfailingly friendly.

10. Shop at Local Markets
Products are generally cheaper at local markets than in supermarkets.

AREA BY AREA

The scenic town of Perast

BAY OF KOTOR

Nothing on the Montenegrin coast compares with the Bay of Kotor (Boka Kotorska). This beautiful natural inlet consists of an outer bay leading to a two-lobed inner bay, shaped like the wings of a butterfly. It's an epic landscape, designated a UNESCO World Heritage Site for both its natural and cultural-historical value. And its history is clear to see. Colourful old towns – like Perast and Kotor – dot the bay's coastline, showcasing the architectural treasures of the Venetian and Ottoman empires that once ruled this desirable maritime area, and attracting a large proportion of Montenegro's tourism. Yet wilder corners still exist. In the rugged mountains that loom over the bay, scenic walks, lonely churches and lesser-known historic sites await.

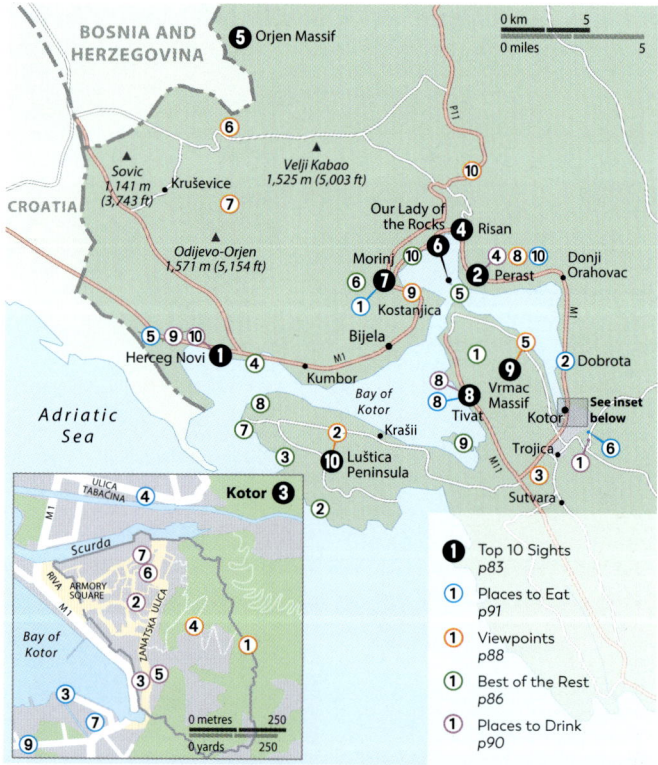

BOSNIA AND HERZEGOVINA
5 Orjen Massif

0 km 5
0 miles 5

6

CROATIA

Sovic 1,141 m (3,743 ft)
Kruševice
7

Velji Kabao 1,525 m (5,003 ft)

10

Odijevo-Orjen 1,571 m (5,154 ft)

Our Lady of the Rocks 4 Risan
Morinj 10 6
6 7 9 2 Perast
1 Kostanjica
Bijela
Herceg Novi 1
5 9 10
4 Kumbor

4 8 10
Donji Orahovac

5

1 5 2 Dobrota
9
Bay of Kotor
8 7 Vrmac Massif
Tivat
Krašii
Luštica Peninsula
9
Kotor See inset below
6
Trojica
1
3
Sutvara

Adriatic Sea

8
7
3
2 10
3
Kotor 3
2

Kotor
ULICA TABACINA 4
Scurda
7
RIVA ARMORY SQUARE 6
2 4
Bay of Kotor 1
5
3 3
7
9

0 metres 250
0 yards 250

For places to stay in this area, see p128

1 Herceg Novi

📍 A3 🏠 Jova Dabovića 12; herceg novi.travel

Perched at the entrance to the Bay of Kotor, Herceg Novi was founded in the 14th century by Tvrtko I, king of Bosnia – a large statue of whom you'll find standing on the waterfront. Today, this historic town is one of the bay's most photogenic, its buildings cascading down the steep hillside to a waterfront promenade, all watched over by the Ottoman-era Kanli Kula fortress. It's worth popping into the fortress for the sweeping views it provides. Other than that, Herceg Novi is a lovely place to linger, with lots of places to eat or sip a coffee as you watch the world go by.

2 Perast

Pretty Perast *(p44)* sits on the northern shore of the Bay of Kotor. While it's a pleasant town to amble around, it's most famous for its iconic view of the Bay of Kotor. From the town's waterfront, the two nearby islets, Our Lady of the Rocks (Gospa od Škrpjela, *p84*) and St George's Island (Sveti Đorđe, *p87*), can be seen against the area's epic mountains.

3 Kotor

The bay's eponymous town *(p32)* is also its star attraction. Founded in the 5th century BCE, Kotor is a wonderfully atmospheric place – a warren of stone-paved alleys meandering between lively squares, enclosed by massive medieval walls. There are numerous highlights here. Kotor Fortress *(p33)* snakes up the hillside, offering awe-inspiring views of the

Herceg Novi's buildings tumbling down the hillside

bay below. There's also the Cathedral of St Tryphon *(p54)*, with its twin bell towers and holy relics of the saint himself. Then there's the charming Cat Museum *(p53)* which is exactly what the name suggests: a museum dedicated to the town's beloved cat population.

4 Risan

📍 B2

The small town of Risan has a history stretching back more than two millennia. It was once a stronghold of the Illyrians, before the Romans swept in during the 3rd century BCE. The latter were responsible for the town's main attraction: a series of Roman floor mosaics *(p52)* dating from the 2nd century CE. They cover a vast area and are all that remains of a significant Roman villa that once stood here.

Well-preserved Roman mosaics in the town of Risan

5 Orjen Massif
⚑ A2 ⊕ orjen.me

High above the western arm of the Bay of Kotor, Orjen is a craggy, heavily karstified mountain area which is much less well-known – and less accessible – than Mount Lovćen (p40). The massif includes several peaks. The best two for hiking are Subra (1,675 m/5,495 ft) in the south, which you can hike to from the Subra Mountain Hut near the village of Kameno, and Zubački Kabao (1,894 m/6,213 ft, also called Orjen) in the north. The latter is located on the border with Bosnia and Herzegovina and is best accessed via the Orjen Saddle road.

6 Our Lady of the Rocks
⚑ B2 ⌂ Offshore from Perast

Known in Montenegrin as Gospa od Škrpjela, this small, artificial island is a short boat-ride from Perast. The seabed on which it stands was raised by local fishers some time in the 15th century. As the story goes, an icon of the Madonna and Child was found in the sea here and locals vowed to create a church to honour its discovery; they began by dumping rocks and sinking old boats loaded with stones to create this tiny island. A church was then built atop it, and it now hosts a small museum, with paintings by Tripo Kokolja, a Baroque artist from Perast.

7 Morinj
⚑ B3

The former fishing village of Morinj stands in lush surroundings beside the sea. It's best known for its old olive mills, where wheat and other grains were ground and olive oil was pressed for some two centuries, before being loaded onto boats. One of the former mills here is now a standout restaurant (Konoba Ćatovića Mlini; p91).

8 Tivat
⚑ B3 🛈 Palih Boraca; tivat.travel

Tivat is the glitz and glamour to Kotor's medieval charm. The area has been inhabited since antiquity but it was transformed in the 2000s by the development of Porto Montenegro. Like a small Monte Carlo dropped on the shores of Montenegro, this contemporary resort features a large, modern marina, an uber-luxurious residential area and a designer retail complex. Visitors come to browse the upmarket boutiques and treat themselves at top-notch restaurants, all while gazing at the phenomenal concentration of superyachts along the marina.

Our Lady of the Rocks, an artificial island near Perast

**The rocky peaks of the
Vrmac Massif**

9 Vrmac Massif
B3

Vrmac is a long, steep-sided ridge dividing the inner and outer parts of the Bay of Kotor – as such, it offers stunning views of both the Adriatic coast and the bay's stunning inland peaks (including Mount Lovćen). The ridge makes for a great hike, starting from the old road above the Vrmac tunnel or from the village of Donja Lastva, near Tivat. Whichever way you pick, you'll pass the old Austro-Hungarian Vrmac Fort and the peak of Sveti Ilija.

10 Luštica Peninsula
B3

The beautiful Luštica Peninsula forms the southern arm of the Bay of Kotor. While part of the peninsula (Luštica Bay, to the south) has been developed into a luxury tourist resort, much of the area remains rugged and wild. Small farms dot the terrain, producing local olive oil and cheese, while inviting little villages (including Klinci and Bjelila) provide low-key accommodation. Hiking trails also weave around the area, taking travellers to scenic coves and beaches – Dobreč (p87) and Žanjic (p86) are popular places to sunbathe.

A DAY IN THE BAY OF KOTOR

Morning

Starting out early to avoid the traffic, drive along the coastal road from **Kotor** (p32) to **Perast** (p44). Spend the early morning in this historic town, taking a boat trip over to the islands of Our Lady of the Rocks and St George and enjoying a coffee on the waterfront. Next, make a pitstop in **Risan** (p83) to visit the spectacular Roman mosaics. Ready for lunch? Settle in at famed restaurant Konoba Ćatovića Mlini (p91), in **Morinj**.

Afternoon

After a delicious feast, hop on the **Kamenari** car ferry to **Lepetane**, on the other side of the bay. Drive towards Tivat but turn inland at Donja Lastva, following the winding road up to **Gornja Lastva** (p86). This pretty village makes for a lovely afternoon wander – don't miss the 15th-century stone church. It's a short drive from here to your next stop: **Tivat**, where the so-called Island of Flowers (connected to the mainland by a short bridge) is a must-visit. Driving out of Tivat, you've got two options: take the tunnel back to Kotor or continue your drive to the **Luštica Peninsula**.

So you've chosen the scenic route? Swoop around the coast of this wild area, peeking at **Rose**'s submarine tunnels (p87) and swimming at beaches like **Žanjic** (p86).

Best of the Rest

1. Gornja Lastva
B3

Set above Tivat (p84) in the hills of the Vrmac peninsula, this red-roofed village is home to a striking 15th-century stone church. Another highlight is the hike to the top of nearby Sveti Ilija, a peak that offers glorious views over the Bay of Kotor and surrounding rugged hills.

2. Blue Cave
B3

Located on the southern shore of the Luštica Peninsula (p85), this large sea cave is famed for its mesmerizing blue hue, created by sunlight reflecting off the sea floor. Boat tours visit the cave, with many departing from Kotor.

3. Žanjic
B3

This pretty stretch of pebble beach on the Luštica Peninsula's southwest coast is deservedly popular. For one thing, the water here is exceptionally clear, making it a great place for snorkelling. For another, it's west facing, meaning excellent sunsets on clear days.

4. Savina Monastery
A3

Just outside Herceg Novi (p83), this monastery is one of the most important on the Montenegrin coast. The complex includes the 11th-century Church of the Assumption, which was rebuilt in the 18th century, and the Great Temple of the Assumption, built in the late 1700s.

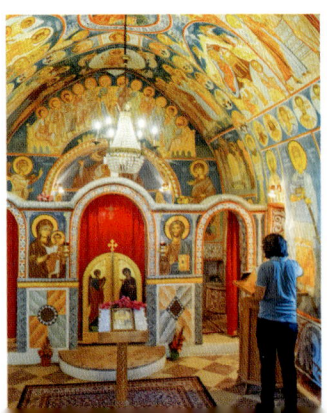

The painted interior of Savina Monastery

The summit of Sveti Ilija,
found above Gornja Lastva

8. Submarine Tunnels, Rose
▣ A3

On either side of the village of Rose are three abandoned submarine tunnels once used by the former Yugoslav Navy. Well protected from the open sea, the tunnels' entrances were hidden from aerial view by fake polystyrene rocks (you can still see these at one of the sites). While it's possible to access some of them on foot, it's best to go by boat.

9. Sveti Marko
▣ B3

Just offshore from Tivat Airport, this small island – historically known as Stradioti – was once a Club Med resort, but was abandoned after the break-up of Yugoslavia. Today, it's regained its popularity thanks to its lush greenery and pretty beach; take a taxi boat over from Tivat to reach it. Nearby is the smaller Island of Flowers, connected to the mainland by a bridge, on which sits a monastery dedicated to the Archangel Michael.

5. St George's Island
▣ B3

This little islet is found close to the more famous Our Lady of the Rocks *(p84)* and, unlike its artificially created neighbour, it's a natural island. Boat tours run from Perast *(p44)* to the isle, which is home to a 12th-century Benedictine monastery.

6. Church of St Elijah
▣ B2

Clinging to the slopes above Morinj *(p84)*, this little church dates from the 15th century. It's a bit of a trek to get there – the easiest way is to drive from Herceg Novi *(p83)*, passing through the villages of Kameno and Mandići, followed by a 20-minute walk up a rough track. Yet it's more than worth the effort, with the church's elevated location commanding impressive views across the Bay of Kotor.

7. Dobreč
▣ A3

While Žanjic tends to draw most of the crowds, this blue-flagged beach shouldn't be underestimated. Found near the tip of the Luštica Peninsula, it features some of the clearest waters on the Montenegrin coast.

10. Lipci Rock Art
▣ B2 ▣ Off the E65

Between Morinj *(p84)* and Risan *(p83)* on the western side of the Bay of Kotor lies a remarkable collection of prehistoric rock art. Thought to date from the Bronze Age, the drawings were discovered in the 1960s and include several stylized deer.

**Depiction of a deer
at Lipci Rock Art**

The spectacular view from the Ladder of Kotor

Viewpoints

1. Ladder of Kotor
B3

An old packhorse route, this broad flight of stone steps leads in 33 relentless switchbacks up above Kotor's Old Town, rising to a height of 900 m (3,000 ft). On the way it takes in incredible panoramas of the town, bay and mountains.

2. Luštica Peninsula Beaches
B3

For great sunsets, look no further than one of the Luštica Peninsula's west-facing beaches. Sandy Plavi Horizonti, framed by pine-clad headlands, is a great option, as is pebbly Žanjic *(p86)*.

3. Kotor Cable Car
B3 **kotorcablecar.com**

Whisking you 1,310 m (4,300 ft) above Kotor in 11 minutes, this cable car offers spectacular views across the town, the bay and the surrounding hills.

4. Our Lady of Remedy
B3

The quintessential view of Kotor is from this chapel, found halfway between the town and Kotor Fortress. From here, the Old Town's terracotta tiled roofs spread out below, enclosed by the wedge-shaped confines of its town walls.

5. Vrmac Ridge
B3

The hike along the Vrmac Ridge, found east of Kotor, promises panoramas of both parts of the mountain-encircled Bay of Kotor.

6. Zubački Kabao
A2

The highest peak of the Montenegrin coastal mountains, Zubački Kabao has sensational vistas of the surrounding tree-sprinkled peaks and green valleys, as well as out towards the sea.

7. Subra
A2

While slightly lower than Zubački Kabao, nearby Subra still offers similar epic views. Plus, its rocky slopes are like a geology textbook come to life, with karst formations dotted here and there.

8. Perast

The waterfront in this pretty town *(p44)* provides lovely vistas across the Bay of Kotor towards the islands of Our Lady of the Rocks and St George.

9. Kostanjica
B3

The rocky beach at the little village of Kostanjica is known for its gorgeous perspective down the length of the inner bay, as well as across towards pretty Perast *(p44)* and its islands.

10. Road to Nikšić
B2

Sweeping along the rugged hills that line the northwestern corner of the Bay of Kotor, the P11 road offers stunning views across the water towards Perast's islands *(p44)*. There's a lay-by where you can park up and take it all in.

Outdoor Activities

1. Swimming
There's no shortage of swimming spots here, whether you're taking a dip off the sandy shores of Plavi Horizonti, jumping into the turquoise waters of the Blue Cave (p86) or having a quiet bathe next to the island of Sveti Marko near Tivat (p87). For a quirkier option, try the submarine tunnels near Rose (p87).

2. Kayaking
If you don't fancy a dip in the sea, consider paddling about in a kayak instead. Kayak Tours Kotor (kayaktours kotor.com/index.php/en) offers one-day tours on the bay, as well as kayak hire if you'd rather strike out on your own.

3. Mountain Biking
After a heart-pumping mountain bike route? Try those found on the Vrmac Massif (p85). If you're looking for something more accessible – and less steep – the 4x4 road between Vrbanj and Orjen Saddle (p84) makes for an excellent run.

4. SUP
A stand-up paddleboard is one of the best ways to explore the Bay of Kotor. SUP Montenegro (supmontenegro.me) offers hire and various tours, including to Sveti Marko, Our Lady of the Rocks (p84) and the submarine tunnels near Rose (p87). There's also a rather wonderful sunset tour available.

5. Sunset Strolls
Whether it's ambling along one of the Luštica Peninsula's beaches or climbing the Ladder of Kotor, there are plenty of great spots for a sunset stroll. Another option is Šetaliste pet Danica, a 5-km (3-mile) waterfront promenade between the towns of Meljine and Igalo that has views of the sun setting over the Adriatic.

6. Road Cycling
There are several good cycling routes around the Bay of Kotor. An excellent, if challenging, choice is the P1 road from Kotor (p32) to Njeguši (p107), which snakes upwards in a relentless series of hairpin bends. Keep an eye out for traffic, as you take in the incredible views across the bay and beyond.

7. Paragliding
Surrounded by mountains, the Bay of Kotor is unsurprisingly a great spot for paragliding. Kotor Paragliding (kotor-paragliding.me) and Paragliding Montenegro (paragliding.me) both offer tandem flights from a launchpad on Lovćen (p40) high above Kotor.

8. Boat Tours
The classic boat tour on the Bay of Kotor includes Our Lady of the Rocks (p84) and the Blue Cave, and generally lasts around three hours. Lots of operators run trips, including Montenegro Submarine (montenegrosubmarine.me).

9. Via Ferrata
Via ferrata routes lace the crags above Kotor's Old Town. Montagna Travel (montagnatravel.me) offers guided climbs, with all equipment supplied and stupendous views guaranteed.

10. Hiking
There's plenty of scope for hiking in the the area, with the Orjen massif (p84) offering some of the best hiking trails on the Montenegrin coast. Highlights include Zubački Kabao and Subra.

Stand-up paddleboarding on the Bay of Kotor

Places to Drink

1. Horizont
C3 **P1 road above Kotor**
Want a drink with a view? Perched at the top of the thrilling Kotor Serpentine road (p68), this terrace bar offers epic panoramas over the Bay of Kotor. Note that payment is in cash only and drink choices can be limited.

2. Jazz Club Evergreen
B3 **Stari Grad 422, Kotor**
Sip cool cocktails and listen to jazz at this lovely, laid-back bar in Kotor's Old Town. There's often live music and, if not, a great soundtrack.

3. Nitrox
B3 **Stari Grad 263, Kotor**
thenitroxpub.com
Located within Kotor's Old Town, Nitrox serves up delicious cocktails, bar snacks and an extensive (if pricey) selection of craft beers. The bar gets busy as the sun sets.

4. Red and White Wine Bar
B2 **Marko Martinovica bb, Perast**
063 216 576
Red and White is arguably the best place in Perast to enjoy a glass of local wine. Go for a five-glass tasting if you're not sure what vintage to choose, and order some prosciutto and other nibbles on the side.

5. Bandiera
B3 **Ulica 2, Kotor**
This small café-bar is located near the Gurdić bastion. It's particularly buzzy in the evening, when cheap drinks draw the crowds in.

6. Old Winery
B3 **Stari Grad 488, Kotor**
068 517 417
This beloved wine bar offers a range of Montenegrin vintages and top-notch Mediterranean food. It's the ideal place to gather with friends after a long day of sightseeing.

7. Bokun
B3 **Ulica 1, Kotor** **069 290 019**
Unwind over a coffee or a pint of beer at this quiet bar on the edge of the Old Town. Prices are very affordable considering its central location.

8. Propela
B3 **Obala Maršala Tita, Tivat**
This popular bar on Tivat's waterfront has plenty of outdoor seating, meaning visitors can watch the world and enjoy the sea breeze, too.

9. Peter's Pie
A3 **Šetalište pet Danica 18, Herceg Novi** **peterspie.com**
This vegetarian café whips up some of Herceg Novi's best smoothies, the perfect remedy for Montenegro's summer heat.

10. Miška
A3 **16 Vasa Ćuhovića, Herceg Novi**
A stylish little café famed for its coffee, Miška is loved by locals. Plant-based milk alternatives are available and there are numerous vegan cakes, too. Get a takeaway cup for a morning walk along the nearby waterfront.

Sweeping views from Horizont, a bar high above Kotor

Places to Eat

PRICE CATEGORIES

For a three-course meal for one, with half a bottle of wine (or equivalent meal), taxes and extra charges.

€ under €15 €€ €15–€25 €€€ over €25

Nevjesta Jadrana Restaurant, with views of the Bay of Kotor

1. Konoba Ćatovića Mlini

B3 · E65, Morinj · catovica-mlini.com · €€€

This landmark restaurant is housed in a renovated former olive mill, in the village of Morinj. There's lots of seafood on the menu, from sea bass *carpaccio* to prawns with courgettes on rice.

2. Konoba Portun

B3 · Dobrota 168 · konobaportun.com · €€€

Just outside Kotor, this well-respected place has tables right by the sea and an emphasis on seafood.

3. Galion

B3 · Šuranj bb, Kotor · galion.me · €€€

With its glassy extension hovering above the bay, Galion has a fairly unbeatable waterfront location. Its menu is equally impressive, with an array of exquisitely prepared seafood.

4. Resto Bar Tanaca

B3 · Tabacina 556, Kotor · taraca.me · €€

If you need a break from Montenegro's multitude of seafood restaurants, head to this popular restaurant. It serves modern dishes such as Buddha bowls and burgers, with vegan options, too.

5. Amber

A3 · Mića Vavića, Topla, Herceg Novi · amber-rest.com · €€

Feast on Georgian cuisine at this characterful restaurant on the coast. Everything on the menu is delicious, so it's worth asking the friendly staff to help you decide.

6. Nevjesta Jadrana Restaurant

C3 · Žanjev do · nevjestajadrana.weebly.com · €€

This good-value restaurant is situated on the edge of the P1 road, near the top of the Kotor Serpentine *(p68)*. Bag a seat on the terrace for photo-worthy views.

7. BBQ Tanjga

B3 · E65, Kotor · 069 863 836 · €

This unassuming spot is arguably the best place in the Bay of Kotor for well-priced, no-nonsense grills.

8. Bokka Modern Restaurant

B3 · Teuta Residences, Tivat · portomontenegro.com/shop-and-dine/bokka-modern · €€€

Located in upscale Porto Montenegro, this elegant restaurant serves up plenty of seafood, as well as other traditional local dishes.

9. Ladovina Kitchen & Wine Bar

B3 · Njegoševa 209, Kotor · ladovina.me · €€€

This Italian spot has a leafy outdoor terrace, tasty food and top-tier wine.

10. Trattoria Rosmarino

B3 · Perast bb · 069 333 227 · €€€

Perfect for a date-night, this romantic trattoria offers picture-perfect views of the bay and beautifully presented food to pair with it.

The scenic town of Perast, in the Bay of Kotor

THE COAST

Montenegro's super-scenic Adriatic coast encompasses its key holiday spots. It's an area dominated by sweeping sandy beaches, quieter coves and buzzy tourist towns – like party hot spot Budva – but there's plenty more to do, too. Budva's magnificent Old Town, the atmospheric ruins of Stari Bar and the 12th-century Gradište Monastery offer a cultural breather after too many days at the beach. Meanwhile, the inland lakes promise the country's best bird-watching opportunities.

1 Budva

Budva (p30) is the party capital of the Montenegrin coast and one of its most popular seaside destinations. It's home to the Budva Riviera – a stretch of coastline from here to Petrovac that includes top beaches like Mogren, Jaz and Ploče. While the beaches, and beach bars, are the main draw for many, Budva also has a beautifully preserved Old Town on the western side of the bay. Here, narrow cobbled streets weave between lively cafés, local restaurants and cool galleries.

●	**Top 10 Sights** p94
①	**Places to Eat** p101
①	**Best of the Rest** p98
①	**Beaches** p100

For places to stay in this area, see p129

2 Pržno
□ C4

Pržno is a former fishing village with a very popular sandy beach (a considerable portion of which is owned by a hotel). While the area immediately behind the beach is fairly built up, further back there's a rugged landscape of olive groves. Pržno is close to several other beaches, including Queen's Beach, so if you can't find a free spot here you have numerous other options.

3 Sveti Stefan
□ C4

This beautiful little island, clustered with old stone houses with terracotta tiled roofs and connected to the mainland by a narrow walkway, is one of the most iconic and glamorous spots on the Adriatic coast. The capital of the local Paštrovići Clan from the 15th to the end of the 18th century, it was converted into a resort in 1960. In 2009, it was transformed into an ultra-luxurious five-star hotel (the Aman Sveti Stefan) and began to attract a host of celebrity guests, including Elizabeth Taylor, Sophia Loren and Brad Pitt. The hotel closed in 2021, and while there's talk of it reopening, for now, its pretty neighbouring beaches – formerly for hotel guests only (day-passes for non-guests were an eye-watering €100) – have been reclaimed by locals.

Terracotta stone houses clustered on the island of Sveti Stefan

Sunbeds lining the beach of Buljarica, on the Budva Riviera

4 Buljarica
□ C4

Buljarica is the largest of the beaches on the Budva Riviera. It's a 2.4 km (1.5 mile) stretch of pebbles with a sandy section in the middle – and without the usual sprawl of development behind it. One of around 20 Blue Flag beaches on this part of the coast, it has plenty of facilities, including sun loungers and parasols, beachfront bars and restaurants. The calmer, northern part is good for families. A path leads along the clifftops to nearby Petrovac.

5 Petrovac
□ C4

Long favoured as a quieter alternative to Budva, Petrovac na More (to give it its full name) seems to be doing its best to catch up with its northern neighbour in terms of tourism. Nevertheless, it's still a beautiful place, with its Venetian-era fortress clinging to a craggy peninsula, its palm tree-lined waterfront promenade and sandy city beach. Nearby Lučice Beach, which looks out to a pair of offshore islets, Katič and Sveta Neđelja, is also popular.

The painted interior of Gradište Monastery

6 Gradište Monastery
C4 ❖ **Kaluđerac**

Founded in 1116, this Serbian Orthodox monastery is located in the village of Kaluđerac, on a hillside above Buljarica beach. A branch of the Dečani Monastery in Kosovo, it consists of three churches, dedicated to St Nicholas, the Assumption of the Virgin Mary and St Sava. St Nicholas is believed to be the oldest of the three, although it owes its current appearance to the 17th century, and contains some beautiful frescoes from 1620.

7 Bar
D5

Montenegro's main port, Bar is generally bypassed by visitors heading for Budva and other more glamorous spots along the coast. And while it's the Old Town, Stari Bar, which is one of Montenegro's must-sees, there are several things of note in Bar itself. The huge Church of St Jovan Vladimir, which was completed in 2016 and is lavishly decorated with frescoes, King Nikola's Palace and the large Selimiye Mosque

are highlights here. Away from the modern boulevards of the town, the nearby Rikavac Canyon is a great place for canyoning.

8 Stari Bar
Stari Bar (Old Bar) *(p36)* is one of Montenegro's most unique sites. Perched on a hillside high above the port of Bar, its rambling old walls enclose the ruins of a medieval town, partly subsumed by greenery and surrounded by ancient olive terraces. While the town may appear lost in time, it remains a lively place. The street running along the old walls is packed with a succession of fantastic restaurants and cafés where Albanian influences are strong and the food is absolutely delicious.

9 Lake Skadar
The largest lake in the Balkans, Lake Skadar *(p26)* stretches across the border into Albania. A vast and incredibly beautiful place, it is encircled by reed beds and surrounded by mountains, while its lake surface is a patchwork of water lilies and water chestnuts. Scenery aside, the lake is a haven for birdlife, with 280 species recorded and around a quarter of a million birds passing through during the winter migration. Virpazar *(p98)* is the main gateway town to tourism on the lake, with a small collection of restaurants and hotels; boat and kayaking tours also leave from the port here. The village of Karuč is also worth

The tiny village of Karuč, on the shores of Lake Skadar

ANCIENT OLIVE TREES

The hills around Stari Bar have been planted with olive trees since the ancient Greeks and Romans were here. One particularly old specimen – known simply as Stara Maslina (old olive tree) – stands in Tomba village and is thought to be around 2,000 years old. It was found to be drying out in 2023 and efforts are now underway to save it.

visiting for its fish restaurants, while the island and medieval monastery of Beška is a striking sight on the lake. The lake is also one of the best places in Montenegro for freshwater swimming.

10 Ulcinj

Once an infamous pirates' lair at the southern end of the Montenegrin coast, Ulcinj *(p42)* is now a wonderfully vibrant place with a beautiful Old Town and stacks of history – its ancient fortress is surrounded by massive walls which plunge into the sea below. Ulcinj's Albanian majority and numerous mosques give it a quite different feel from other towns on the coast, and the nearby Ulcinj saltpans *(p99)*, Velika Plaža *(p100)* and Ada Bojana *(p98)* are some of the highlights of the Montenegrin Adriatic.

A DAY ON THE SOUTHERN MONTENEGRIN COAST

Morning

Pack your suncream and your swimsuit: it's time to hit the coast. Starting your drive in **Budva** *(p30)*, follow the seaside south, passing coastal resorts such as **Sveti Stefan** *(p95)* and **Petrovac** *(p95)* – you're spoiled for beaches on this drive, but aim for a morning dip before the crowds descend. At **Bar** turn inland and visit **Stari Bar** *(p36)* – the perfect spot for a traditional lunch – then return to the coast and continue to **Ulcinj** *(p42)*.

Afternoon

You could drive back up the coast the way you came, but then you'd be missing out on this area's inland treasures. En route to **Lake Skadar** *(p26)*, make a detour to visit **Lake Šas** *(p99)* – a miniature version of Montenegro's most famous lake, with many of the same bird species. From here, swing over to **Štegvaš** for your first views of stunning Lake Skadar. Continue along the southern shore of the lake by way of **Ostros**, **Murići** (where there's a lovely beach; *p100*) and Godinje *(p98)* (where you can have a drink at **Paradise Food and Wine**; *p101*), to **Virpazar** *(p98)*. Stop here to join a tranquil boat trip on the lake. Finally, it's time to return to Budva, either through the Sozina tunnel or the scenic road above it.

Best of the Rest

1. Virpazar
⚐ D4

The village of Virpazar is the main gateway to the Crmnica wine region and Lake Skadar (*p26*), where visitors can explore the stunning landscapes of Lake Skadar National Park. Highlights include the old stone bridge, and the ruins of the medieval Besac fortress, set high above the town.

2. Ada Bojana
⚐ E6

At the southernmost point on the Montenegrin coast, divided from Albania by one arm of the River Bojana, Ada Bojana is a small wedge-shaped island known for its rustic seafood restaurants, Robinson Crusoe-like feel, and large naturist camp. A footbridge crosses to the island from Velika plaža.

3. Sveti Nikola
⚐ C4

This elongated island, the largest on the Montenegrin coast, lies just offshore from Budva's Old Town. Known locally (perhaps optimistically) as Hawaii, the uninhabited island has a distinctive, lopsided profile, and features fallow deer and many small beaches.

4. Godinje
⚐ D4

Nestled in the hills above Lake Skadar is this small village, just 5 km (3 miles) from Virpazar. Godinje was depopulated after the huge 1979 earthquake, but has experienced a resurgence over the past decade and now has some lovely family-run guesthouses and tasty eateries.

5. Rumija
⚐ D5

If you only hike one mountain on the Montenegrin coast, Rumija is the one. The 1,592-m (5,223-ft) mountain has fabulous views from the summit – overlooking the Adriatic on one side and Lake Skadar on the other, with the huge, brooding peaks of Prokletije on the Albanian border beyond. There's an easy hiking trail to the top from Stari Bar, and a small church on the summit that was airlifted there by helicopter.

6. Praskvica Monastery
⚐ C4 ⚑ Jadranska magistrala bb

First mentioned in the early 14th century, this Serbian Orthodox monastery is located in Čelobrdo, a village on the hillsides above Sveti Stefan (*p95*). Half a dozen churches

belong to Praskvica – two here at the monastery (dedicated to the Holy Trinity and to St Nicholas), and four down on the island of Sveti Stefan.

7. Crmnica
🗺 D4

The landscape around Virpazar and Lake Skadar is home to Montenegro's best wine region. Crmnica is the place to try full-bodied red wines made from the local black-skinned Vranac grape, Montenegro's main variety, at family-run vineyards, accompanied by a tasty local cheese and charcuterie platter. The easiest way to arrange a wine tour of the area is through a local agency or your accommodation in Virpazar.

8. Ulcinj Saltpans
🗺 E6

These saltpans, the largest on the Adriatic, are among the most important areas for birdlife on the Montenegrin coast. Over 250 species have been recorded here including Dalmatian pelican, spoonbill and flamingo, and the area is a major stopover on migration routes. Despite the area being recognized as a RAMSAR wetland site in 2019, years of decay following the bankruptcy of the salt works in 2013 has left this incredible habitat in disrepair.

A flock of flamingos at the Ulcinj saltpans

9. The Coastal Traversal
🗺 A2–D5

Stretching from Orjen in the north to Rumija in the south, the Montenegrin Coastal Traversal (known locally as the PPT) is a 138-km (85-mile) hiking and mountain-biking trail taking in the highest mountain scenery along the coast. Hiking the whole trail is possible but some stages are not clearly marked and accommodation can be scarce. Local tour operators, such as Zalaz (*zalaz.me*), offer a variation on the route taking in some of the best sections, with transfers at relevant points.

10. Lake Saš
🗺 E6

Lake Saš (Saško jezero in Montenegrin, Liqeni I Shasit in Albanian) is a small lake just 1 km (less than a mile) from the Albanian border, between the shores of Lake Skadar and Ulcinj. Like the much larger Lake Skadar, it's a great spot for bird-watching, and the neighbouring town of Svač has a long history – it was an important centre in medieval times, and the nearby archaeological site has ruins of churches and other buildings.

The old stone bridge in the picturesque village of Virpazar

Aerial view of Velika Plaža beach

Beaches

1. Ada Bojana (Ulcinj)
📍 E6

At the southern tip of the Montenegrin coast, this island between two arms of the River Bojana is a sandy paradise. It's mostly a naturist area, though there is an area for clothed visitors as well.

2. Velika Plaža (Ulcinj)
📍 E6

Velika Plaža lives up to its name of "big beach" – its sweeping stretch of golden sand makes it the longest beach in the country. It's also one of Montenegro's best spots for kitesurfing.

3. Ladies' beach (Ulcinj)
📍 E6

Originally this beach was popular due to its sulphur springs, which were said to bring health benefits. Today, the small rocky cove is a women-only space.

4. Crystal Beach (Utjeha Hladna Uvala)
📍 D5

This shingle beach can only be reached via a steep trail or by boat from Ulcinj. The tranquil setting, backed by steep rocky cliffs, makes it all worthwhile.

5. Mogren (Budva)
📍 C4

Located just west of Budva's Old Town are these two beaches connected by a tunnel through the rocky headland. Make the walk to the second beach to enjoy a less crowded, tranquil space.

6. Murići (Lake Skadar)
📍 D4

Follow the narrow winding road 22 km (13 miles) from Virpazar and you'll find this beautiful beach on the southern shore of Lake Skadar (p26).

7. Drobni Pijesak (Rijeka Reževići)
📍 C4

Lying roughly midway between Sveti Stefan and Petrovac is this nice shingle beach with calm water, sun loungers for hire and a couple of restaurants.

8. Lučice (Petrovac)
📍 C4

Within easy walking distance of Petrovac, this popular sandy beach is protected by a headland.

9. Perazića Do (Petrovac)
📍 C4

Follow the path from Petrovac through pine trees and several tunnels to find the almost fantasy-like Perazića Do beach. This beautiful, 40-m (130-ft) pebble beach, overlooked by a massive abandoned hotel at one end, has some of the country's clearest waters, lush vegetation and towering cliffs.

10. Jaz (Budva)
📍 C4

Jaz is understandably popular. This long arc of sparkling sand is enclosed by verdant headlands and located within easy reach of Budva.

Places to Eat

1. Grape Café
📍 C4 🏠 Ulica Babilonija 112, Budva
📞 067 612 838 · €€

Expect reasonable prices and a range of dishes at this popular little café.

2. Konoba Bocun
📍 C4 🏠 Ulica Mimoza 177, Budva
📞 069 514 879 · €€

Away from Budva's beaches, you'll find this excellent restaurant offering grilled Montenegrin fare, done to perfection.

3. Restoran Kaldrma
📍 D5 🏠 Starobarsha čarsija bb, Stari Bar 📞 067 846 404 · €€

This wonderful little restaurant, on the street outside the walls of Stari Bar, serves up delicious traditional dishes with heaps of character.

4. Konoba Demidžana
📍 D4 🏠 Virpazar bb 📞 066 133 387 · €€

Expect perfectly cooked carp and other freshwater fish at this rustic spot, right next to the old stone bridge in Virpazar.

5. Paradise Food and Wine
📍 D4 🏠 Godinje bb, Virpazar
📞 068 552 223 · €€

Take a seat on the terrace of this village restaurant to enjoy breathtaking views

over Lake Skadar while sampling tasty fare produced by its organic farm.

6. Konoba Bedem
📍 D5 🏠 Starobarsha čarsija bb, Stari Bar 📞 069 666 336 · €€

Feast on some of the best authentic Montenegrin dishes at this homely spot, decorated with cosy cushions and brightly painted walls.

7. Restaurant Dulcinea
📍 E6 🏠 Stari Grad bb, Ulcinj
📞 069 267 756 · €€

This family-run place in Ulcinj's Old Town has been serving great-value local food since 1984.

8. Restaurant Antigona
📍 E6 🏠 Stari Grad bb, Ulcinj
📞 069 154 117 · €€

Places like Antigona are popular for a reason. It combines a fabulous location on the terrace above the waterfront with sumptuous food, all at very reasonable prices.

9. Ćićkova čarda
📍 E6 🏠 Ada Bojana 📞 068 018 140 · €€€

The freshest of seafood is paired with well-chosen domestic wines to create the perfect meal at Ćićkova čarda. This idyllic spot is right beside the River Bojana where it flows into the Adriatic.

10. Konoba Kod Ranka
📍 E6 🏠 Ada Bojana 📞 069 797 676 · €€€

Take a seat at this traditional coastal restaurant to enjoy freshly caught sea bass, prawns or fish soup.

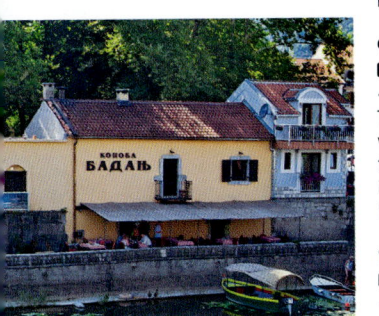

Konoba Demidžana, a popular seafood spot in Virpazar

CENTRAL MONTENEGRO

Montenegro's tourism may be concentrated in the mountains and along the coast, but its central region still has plenty to offer. Big cities dominate this area: there's Podgorica (the capital that receives fewer visitors than it deserves), the historic former capital, Cetinje, and the country's second-largest city, Nikšić. Top museums, great restaurants and fascinating cultural institutions are scattered across these three urban centres. But of course, this being Montenegro, the mountains are never far away. Lovćen National Park offers near-boundless scope for outdoor adventure, while Ostrog Monastery, precariously perched on a cliff face, is a must-visit centre of religion.

●	Top 10 Sights	p103
①	Places to Eat	p109
①	Best of the Rest	p106
①	Walks	p108

For places to stay in this area, see p130

1 Ostrog Monastery

Ostrog Monastery *(p48)* stands in a spectacular setting: built into the face of a sheer cliff some 700 m (2,296 ft) above the valley floor, its white, fortress-like façade contrasts with the warm hues of the rocks surrounding it. Founded in the early 17th century by Vasilije Jovanović, Bishop of Zahumlje and Herzegovina (later glorified as Basil of Ostrog), it was partly rebuilt in the 1920s following a destructive fire. Still a working monastery, the site attracts a large number of pilgrims (who you'll often see walking barefoot between the Upper and Lower monasteries). There's no bus here, but taxis cover the route – note that if you're driving, the road from Danilovgrad is the less vertiginous option.

Ostrog Monastery's striking façade, bathed in a warm light

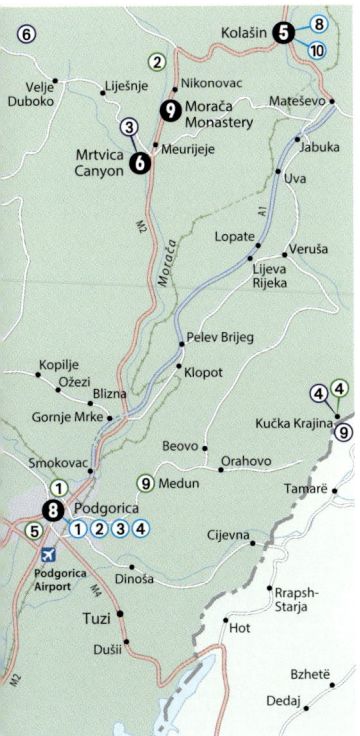

2 Cetinje

Cetinje *(p46)*, Montenegro's erstwhile royal capital – Podgorica didn't gain the title until after World War II – was founded in 1482 and stands in a rolling, rocky landscape below Mount Lovćen. It has remained a relatively quiet place, with a rich sense of history and grand buildings that reflect the town's former status.

3 Lovćen National Park

A national park since 1952, Mount Lovćen *(p40)* is a prominent peak dividing the Bay of Kotor from Cetinje. Its 1,657-m (5,436-ft) summit provides a suitably spectacular setting for the mausoleum of Petar II Petrović-Njegoš *(p41)*, ruler of Montenegro from 1830 to 1851. An asphalt road leads up to just below the mausoleum.

4 Nikšić

🅿 C1 🚋 10 Ivana Milutinovića

Montenegro's second city may be a major industrial centre but it's also home to several museums and cultural institutions, as well as a large student population. Sights include the so-called Tzar's Bridge (Carev Most), an 18-arch stone bridge built in the 19th century, and the former Palace of King Nikola (now the Heritage Museum). Montenegro's largest brewery is also located in Nikšić, producing the eponymous Nikšićko beer.

5 Kolašin
🅟 M5 🅟 M9 road

An outdoor adventure capital to rival Žabljak (p116), Kolašin stands on the doorstep of several beautiful mountain areas. Biogradska Gora National Park (p113), Bjelasica (site of the country's best ski resort; p117), the Mrtvica Canyon and the Sinjajevina mountains are all within easy reach from town.

6 Mrtvica Canyon
🅟 E1

Southwest from Kolašin lies the Mrtvica Canyon, a sheer-sided gorge that looms above the turquoise Morača River. It's an incredibly wild spot, reaching over 1,000 m (3,280 ft) deep in places, with plenty of lush vegetation and mostly unmarked trails. At one point, the path follows a gallery cut through the face of a sheer cliff, created by the former Yugoslav People's Army. There's also an old stone bridge (Danilov Most) partway up the canyon, built by Prince Danilo I Petrović-Njegoš in memory of his mother.

7 Rijeka Crnojevića
🅟 D3 🆆 rijekacrnojevica.me

Rijeka Crnojevića is a small settlement on the river of the same name, which flows into Lake Skadar (p26). Historically, it was a place of importance – Obod on the opposite bank was the centre of the medieval ruler Ivan Crnojević's realm before he founded Cetinje, and one of the earliest

printing presses in southeast Europe was located here in 1493. These days, however, it's a decidedly laid-back corner of the country, which you'll visit for three things: the view of the "old bridge", a much photographed double-arched stone bridge dating from the 1850s; the restaurants which nestle close beside the river, with plenty of freshwater fish on the menu; and the jaw-dropping view of the river a little way downstream from here, where it turns in a whopping great hairpin.

8 Podgorica
🅟 E3 🆔 47 Slobode; podgorica.travel

Many visitors pass Podgorica by, but the Montenegrin capital has a lot to shout about. It hosts numerous cultural sights and some of the country's best

---

FIERY FRESCOES

Podgorica's epic cathedral is best known for its floor-to-ceiling frescoes; epic as they are, some are decidedly controversial. Among the panoply of saints, look out for the portraits of Communist figures Tito, Karl Marx and Friedrich Engels (all of whom were ideologically opposed to the church) clearly depicted in Hell.

The Cathedral of the Resurrection of Christ, Podgorica

restaurants and bars. Take a stroll through the cobbled streets of the Old Town and you'll soon get waylaid at a wine bar or traditional restaurant like Pod Volat *(p109)* or Lanterna *(p109)*. In terms of cultural landmarks, there's the old Clock Tower (one of the few Ottoman sites that survived bombing in World War II), the small but mighty Museum of Contemporary Art and the dazzling Cathedral of the Resurrection of Christ (its interior is an art gallery in itself; *p54*).

9 Morača Monastery
📍 E1

Founded in 1252 by Stefan Vukanović, of Serbia's Nemanjić dynasty, this monastery is one of the most historically and artistically important pieces of architecture in Montenegro. Built in the style of the Raška School – it features a Romanesque portal, large, single-nave interior and remarkably well-preserved frescoes from the 13th century.

10 Lipa Cave
📍 C3 🕐 May–Oct: daily tours at 10am, 11.30am, 1pm, 2.30pm & 4pm; Apr & Nov: daily tours at 10am, 12pm & 2pm 🌐 lipa-cave.me 🚻♿

Thanks to its karst landscape, Montenegro features a number of spectacular cave systems, but Lipa Cave is undoubtedly the best. Opened to the public in 2015, it's covered with well-maintained concrete paths with plenty of stalactites and stalagmites.

The view of the river bend near Rijeka Crnojevića

A DAY IN CENTRAL MONTENEGRO

Morning
Though relatively short, the drive from **Cetinje** *(p46)* to the edge of **Lake Skadar** *(p26)* is one of the most memorable in Montenegro. Take the old road, passing **Lipa Cave** – it's worth popping in if you have time – towards **Rijeka Crnojevića**. This friendly settlement is a great place for lunch; bag a table at **Konoba Stari Most** *(p109)*, a long-standing local favourite with beautiful views. After food, drive a little way beyond Rijeka Crnojevića and you'll reach the view to end all views: a prominent bend on the river with the vast watery landscape of Lake Skadar beyond.

Afternoon
Leaving the lake, make your way to **Podgorica**, but don't stop in the capital yet. First, you've got to choose your afternoon adventure. Option one involves taking the old road up north to **Morača Monastery** an architectural treasure trove, and the **Mrtvica Canyon**, which promises an incredible hike. Option two takes you through Danilovgrad to the epic **Ostrog Monastery** *(p48)*, one of Montenegro's more important religious sites. Whichever route you choose, drive home via Podgorica, making a stop for dinner at buzzy **Pod Volat** *(p109)*.

Best of the Rest

**Looking across the ruins
of the town of Doclea**

1. Doclea
🅟 E3
Originally an Illyrian settlement, Doclea grew into a large town during the Roman era; later, under Byzantine rule, it became the seat of a bishopric. Destroyed during various invasions in the 4th and 5th centuries, and then hit by a huge earthquake, the site is now in ruins, but it remains an atmospheric spot.

2. Moračke Planine
🅟 E1
This vast, sprawling massif west of the River Morača is much less visited than Durmitor National Park (p22), but is nevertheless a fantastic area for hiking and mountain biking. Along with the Mrtvica Canyon (p104), highlights include the rocky wilderness of the Maganik mountains and the Kapetanevo jezero, a deep lake surrounded by lush pasture and looming mountains.

3. Crvnena Stijena
🅟 A1 🆆 crvenastijena.org
Translating as "red cave", this little-visited site is found near the village of Petrovići, close to the Bosnian border. Excavations at the cave, which is situated in a rather spectacular reddish cliff overlooking Lake Bileć, have revealed archaeological remains

stretching back 70,000 years, from the Late Bronze Age to the Middle Paleolithic era. Nearby is the stone-built Kosijerevo Monastery, which is scenically set on the banks of the Trebišnjica River.

4. Kučka Krajina
🅟 F2
Close to the border with Albania, Kučka Krajina is an excellent yet off-the-radar hiking area, with plenty of rugged peaks and tranquil lakes. Access is via the village of Veruša, where there is a small number of rural guesthouses providing accommodation for those who venture here.

5. Dajbabe Monastery
🅟 E3
On the southern outskirts of Podgorica (p104), the fairly conventional twin-towered façade of this monastery conceals a remarkable cave-church. It was founded in 1897 by the monk Simeon Popović, who continued to paint the interior of the church up until his death in 1941.

**The cave-church inside
Dajbabe Monastery**

The Memorial to the Fallen of the Lješanska Nahija Region

6. Njeguši
🅠 C3
Found on the road from Cetinje *(p46)* to Kotor *(p32)*, this little village has two claims to fame. Firstly, it was the birthplace of the Montenegrin ruler-poet Petar II Petrović-Njegoš *(p41)*, and secondly, it is the place where Montenegro's finest *pršut* (prosciutto) is produced *(p72)*.

7. Krupac Jezero and Slano Jezero
🅠 C1
These artificial lakes were created when nearby Perućica –the first hydroelectric power plant in Montenegro – was built in the 1950s and 60s. The landscape is quite beautiful, particularly that of Lake Slano, with its rocky islets, and both lakes are popular spots for swimming, with several beaches dotted here and there. There are also a handful of playgrounds and places to hire kayaks (making it great for families), plus a shoreside restaurant at Lake Krupac.

8. World War II Monuments
🅠 C1, E3, B2
Montenegro has several prominent *spomeniks* (memorials) to Partisan fighters and civilians killed by Hitler's and Mussolini's forces during World War II. Often conceived on a massive scale, these sombre concrete monuments are incredibly impressive. Those in central Montenegro include the Monument to the Fallen Soldiers on Sutjeska, east of Nikšić *(p103)*, and the Memorial to the Fallen of the Lješanska Nahija Region at Barutana, found southwest of Podgorica *(p104)*. Another impressive *spomenik* is the Monument to Sava Kovačević at Grahovo, around 45 km (30 miles) west of Nikšić.

9. Medun
🅠 E3
Perched on a spectacular crag near Podgorica, Medun was an Illyrian stronghold in the 3rd and 4th centuries BCE. The Ottomans built a fortress here in medieval times and today the fragmented ruins of this archaeological site mostly date from that period. Medun is also home to the grave of Marko Miljanov, a 19th-century Montenegrin statesman, writer and local clan chief, who was born here.

10. Vranjina
🅠 D4
Vranjina is an island off the northern shore of Lake Skadar *(p26)*, around which the two arms of the River Morača curve. The island is home to a tiny village, also named Vranjina, which sits just south of the M2, the main road that connects the island to the mainland. South of the village is a 296-m (971-ft) conical hill, offering gorgeous views across the lake, and a striking church, part of a former monastery.

Walks

1. Jezerski Vrh (Lovćen)
🅿 C3

The main trail to this peak winds up from the rest stop at Ivanova Korita to reach the mausoleum of Petar II Petrović-Njegoš at the top (p41). The view from the platform is sensational.

2. Babina Glava (Lovćen)
🅿 C3

This lesser-known Lovćen trail is an easy loop south from Ivanova Korita to the 1,474-m- (4,835-ft-) peak of Babina Glava.

3. Mrtvica Canyon
🅿 E1

Hiking through the Mrtvica Canyon (p104) is beautiful. The trail follows the left bank of the river, but you can vary the return journey by following the right bank for part of the way – or continue to Kapetanevo Jezero, a scenic lake.

4. Kučka Krajina
🅿 F2

One of the best hikes in this little-known mountain area goes from Bukurmirsko Jezero to Štitan. Note that the trail can be rough and is only partly marked.

5. Kapetanevo Jezero
🅿 C1

The scenic route to Kapetanevo Jezero ("captain's lake") rewards walkers with

The glacial lake of Kapetanevo Jezero

great views of this glacial lake on the plateau of Moračke Planine (p106).

6. Stožac
🅿 C1

Stožac is a 2,141-m (7,024-ft) peak near Kapetanovo Jezero, with stunning views from the summit.

7. Slano Jezero
🅿 C1

This large artificial lake west of Nikšić (p103) is a nice area for hiking and has plenty of opportunities to stop for a refreshing swim.

8. Ostrog Monastery on Foot
🅿 D1

Walking from the lower to the upper part of Ostrog Monastery (p48) is a popular pilgrimage – but you can also walk up to the lower monastery from the local train station. Allow at least an hour for the journey; the path is rocky, but rewarding.

9. Via Dinarica
🅿 F2

Encompassing the Western Balkans, this mega-trail skirts past the mountains of Kučka Krajina in Montenegro then continues into Albania.

10. Obodska Pećina
🅿 D3

To avoid the big peaks, this easy hike from Rijeka Crnojevića (p104) to Obodska Pećina cave is a great option.

Places to Eat

The charmingly rustic interior of Lanterna

1. Lanterna
🗺 E3 🏠 Kralja Nikola 36, Podgorica
🌐 lanterna.me/en · €€€
Lanterna is a very good traditional restaurant in the Old Town, with pastas, salads and traditional dishes such as *kačamak*. It has a rustic interior with a few contemporary updates.

2. Pod Volat
🗺 E3 🏠 Trg Vojvode Bećira Osmanagića 1, Podgorica 📞 069 618 633 · €€
Great food, plenty of character, decent prices: this iconic restaurant ticks all the boxes. Join locals as they pop in for a delicious lunch enjoyed under the canopy of a massive linden tree.

3. Wine bar Bucca
🗺 E3 🏠 Bahu 140, Podgorica 📞 067 991 100 · €€€
Bucca is the best wine bar in town, with a huge range of local and international wines, good food (including some vegetarian options) and a very stylish modern interior.

4. Restoran Porto
🗺 E3 🏠 Bulevar Stanha Dragojevića 40, Podgorica 📞 063 223 303 · €€€
Tucked away on the north side of town, Restoran Porto has Mediterranean dishes and nice decor – picture plenty of greenery, a fountain and olive trees.

5. Restoran Verige
🗺 C3 🏠 Mojhovačha 23, Cetinje
🌐 verige.me · €
Located on the north side of Cetinje, this is a good-value, local favourite specializing in grilled meat.

6. Restoran Belveder
🗺 C3 🏠 Stari put, Cetinje 📞 067 569 217 · €€
On the road to the Lipa Cave and Rijeka Crnojevica, this landmark traditional restaurant has a lovely setting.

7. Konoba Stari Most
🗺 D3 🏠 Rijeha Crnojevića · €€€
One of two original restaurants near the old bridge, Konoba serves up delicious fish and has a lovely setting beside the river.

8. Restaurant Vodenica
🗺 M5 🏠 Breze, Kolašin 📞 067 450 413 · €€
Vodenica is a good-value traditional restaurant on the banks of the Kolašinska stream, with dishes such as roast lamb, trout and *cicvara* (a cheese and cornflour concoction).

9. Restoran Savina Luka
🗺 D3 🏠 Rijeha Crnojevića · €€
Expect a warm welcome and plenty of freshwater fish on the menu at this waterside restaurant.

10. Konoba Nisović
🗺 M5 🏠 Trg Vuhmana Kruščića 14, Kolašin 🌐 foodbooh.me/en/profile/honoba-nisavic-holasin · €€
Opened in 1903, this traditional restaurant is right in the town's centre.

Clockwise from top
**Moraca Monastery;
a row of bells at the
monastery; a mosaic
of Mary and Jesus**

NORTHERN AND EASTERN MONTENEGRO

Welcome to the wild heart of Montenegro. The northern and eastern areas of the country promise an otherworldly landscape of soaring mountains, racing rivers, beautiful lakes and views so big they'll take your breath away. It's here that you'll find three of the country's five national parks – Durmitor, Prokletije and Biogradska Gora – along with more gorges than you can count. Unsurprisingly, this is the best area in the country for hiking, plus numerous other outdoor activities.

For places to stay in this area, see p131

Crno Jezero (Black Lake), a popular swimming spot

1 Durmitor National Park

The Durmitor massif is a huge, sprawling plateau in the north of the country which encompasses soaring mountain peaks and beautiful lakes. Easily accessible, with a huge variety of hiking trails, this is Montenegro's most popular hiking area. A UNESCO World Heritage Site since 1980, Durmitor National Park *(p22)* was founded in 1952 and covers a huge portion of the plateau. Highlights include the stunning Crno Jezero and Škrčko Jezero lakes and the peaks of Međed ("the bear ") and Bobotov Kuk *(p59)* – usually described as the highest peak in Montenegro, although Maja Kolata in Prokletije is slightly higher. The gateway to the park is the busy little mountain town of Žabljak *(p116)*.

2 Crno Jezero

K3 **3 km (2 miles) from Žabljak**

One of the most photographed spots in Durmitor, Black Lake lies just outside Žabljak and offers breathtaking views of the high peaks reflected in its calm surface. The lake is surrounded by dark pine forest and a lovely walking trail.

3 Tara River Canyon

K3

As it carves its way across the eastern side of the Durmitor plateau, the Tara River flows through one of the world's deepest canyons, reaching up to 1,300 m (4,265 ft) deep in places. It's a spectacular sight and its lower course is a hugely popular spot for rafting.

4 Biogradska Gora National Park

M5 **Biogradsko Jezero**

Lower in altitude than the soaring limestone peaks of Durmitor and Prokletije, Biogradska Gora centres on a beautiful lake (Biogradsko Jezero), surrounded by dense, primeval forest. You can hire rowing boats on the lake or follow the easy path around it. Above the forest, the landscape rises to the gently rolling highlands, glacial lakes and rocky knolls of the Bjelasica mountains.

Gleaming gold decorations in the grand Piva Monastery

5 Piva Monastery
📍 J4 🏛 Stolac

The Church of the Assumption of the Holy Mother of God, often simply called the Piva Monastery, is one of the most significant Orthodox churches in Montenegro. It was built in 1573–86, when much of the country was part of the Ottoman Empire; the main frescoes followed in the early years of the 17th century. The size of the church and the fine quality of its decoration are partly explained by the fact that its founder, Bishop Savatije Sokolović, was the brother of the Ottoman Grand Vizier Mehmed Sokolović. The church originally stood on lower ground nearby, but was dismantled and rebuilt in its present location in 1982, following the construction of the Mratinje dam in 1975.

6 Piva Canyon
📍 J3

The River Piva runs across northwestern Montenegro, before flowing into the Drina River in Bosnia. Its eponymous canyon is flooded for around 45 km (28 miles) of its length by Lake Piva, an extraordinary turquoise body of water created by the Mratinje dam. Surrounded by verdant mountain slopes, this is one of the best places in Montenegro for whitewater rafting.

7 Komovi
📍 N4

Small but perfectly formed, Komovi is a group of three mountains, clustered near the border with Albania. It's easy enough to get here by the old road between Andrijevica and Kolašin, which runs across the Trešnjavik Saddle – or better still, you can hike here from Biogradska Gora *(p113)*, following part of the Via Dinarica *(p108)*.

8 Plav
📍 P5

The small town of Plav sits beside a large glacial lake of the same name, surrounded by the Prokletije mountains. The town has a sizeable Albanian population and is predominantly Muslim, with several mosques and an old fortified tower house. The pretty Ali Pasha springs and hiking trails in the scenic Grbaja Valley are nearby.

9 Prokletije National Park
📍 P5 ℹ️ Ali Pasha St, Gusinje 🌐

A swathe of spiky peaks, the Prokletije mountains run along the remote borders between Montenegro, Albania and Kosovo. The name means "the accursed mountains", but don't let that put you off, this is an incredibly beautiful and unspoiled landscape. The area is protected as Prokletije National Park on the Montenegrin side of the border, with further national parks on the Albanian side. The two main access points are the Grbaja Valley and the

The piercing peaks of the Prokletije mountains

KATUNI

Walking in Montenegro's mountains you'll see plenty of small wooden cottages called *katuni*. These settlements are used during the summer by villagers who tend livestock in the high pastures. While many have been abandoned, plenty are still in use: in the Prokletije mountains several have been linked to form a thematic Katun Road (*katunroads.me*).

Ropojana Valley, running from the villages of Gusinje and Vusanje, from where hiking trails lead into the wilds.

10 Peaks of the Balkans

P5 peaksofthebalkans.info

This epic, long-distance hiking trail in the Prokletije mountains meanders along the Balkan borders. The scenery is unforgettable, trails are well marked for the most part and there's accommodation in family-run guesthouses in villages high up among the summer pastures. However, bear in mind that it's very remote (and often snowy) in places and, as it's a trans-border hike, you need a permit – it's easiest to apply for this through a local tour operator like Zbulo (*zbulo.org*).

A DAY IN NORTHERN MONTENEGRO

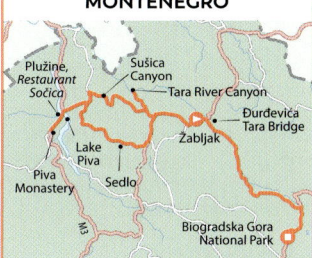

Morning

While you could speed up north on the modern motorway from Podgorica towards Serbia, you'd miss a lot of great scenery. Take the older roads instead, and you're in for a treat. Starting from the popular mountain base of **Žabljak** (*p116*), follow the northern part of the Durmitor Ring anti-clockwise, stopping to take in the breathtaking viewpoints over the **Tara** (*p113*) and **Sušica** (*p117*) canyons. Then, continue through Trsa to beautiful **Lake Piva**, where you can take an hour or so to unwind and fill up on food at the lakeside **Restaurant Sočica** (*p119*).

Afternoon

Come afternoon, head through **Plužine** to visit the historic **Piva Monastery**. After taking in the stunning frescoes here, return to Žabljak on the southern half of the Durmitor Ring, via **Sedlo**, from where there are lovely views of the Durmitor massif. This would make for a nice easy day with plenty of time for stops and cautious driving along the winding roads. If, however, you wish to extend your drive, continue from Žabljak towards the **Đurđevića Tara Bridge** (*p116*), and end your trip in the beautiful **Biogradska Gora National Park** (*p113*).

Best of the Rest

1. Nevidio Canyon
K4

Sheer-sided, narrow and still relatively unknown (the name means "unseen"), this small canyon on the Komarnica River was only discovered in the 1960s. Since then, it's become one of the best places in Montenegro to try canyoning (nevidio-canyoning.com).

2. Grebaje Valley
N5

Running southwest from the village of Gusinje, this spectacular valley marks the border with Albania. It bristles with craggy, snow-tipped peaks – sporting suitably intimidating names like Očnjak (meaning "fang"). Travellers can take in the scenery from the valley floor or head up to Volušnica, a peak on the western side with epic views.

3. Đurđevića Tara Bridge
L3

The Đurđevića Tara Bridge is a hulking concrete arch bridge spanning the Tara River. At the time of its construction in the late 1930s, it was one of the largest bridges of its kind in Europe. The central arch was blown up by a local engineer to block the Italian advance in World War II (he was captured by the Italians and later executed for the act).

Towering Tara Bridge, which spans the eponymous canyon

Pljevlja's Husein Pasha Mosque, its minaret piercing the sky

4. Pljevlja
L2

Not far from the Serbian border, this small town is dominated by its massive coal mine and coal-fired power station. Yet industry isn't all that Pljevlja offers. Sights in town include the Husein Pasha Mosque, built in the late 16th century, and the pretty Holy Trinity Monastery, which dates from around the 15th century. The Homeland Museum Pljevlja is also worth visiting for its archaeological and ethnographic collections, the latter drawn from the treasury of the Holy Trinity Monastery.

5. Žabljak
K3 ⓦtozabljak.com

The gateway to Durmitor National Park (p22), Žabljak is a busy mountain town with plenty of facilities, from hotels, guesthouses and campsites to restaurants and small supermarkets; there's also a shop selling outdoor gear. Some of the most popular hikes in Durmitor start from here, and the village is easily reached by bus from the coast or from Podgorica.

6. Sušica Canyon
⚑ J3

While the Tara Canyon sees flocks of visitors, the Sušica is much less well known. Running north from the high peaks of central Durmitor to join the Tara, it has a beautiful, elongated lake – but you'll need to arrive early in the season to see it as it dries up by mid-summer. There are jaw-dropping views of the canyon from Nedajno village.

7. Bjelasica
⚑ N3

Stretching from Biogradska Gora National Park *(p113)* to the peaks of Komovi, this mountain range is characterized by weathered peaks and sweeping grasslands. There's plenty of scope for hiking and cycling here, away from the crowds of Durmitor.

8. Rožaje
⚑ Q3

This scenically situated town sits on the Ibar River, with roads forking out to two of Montenegro's neighbours: Serbia and Kosovo. It's the largest Bosniak settlement in Montenegro and hosts a variety of sights. The Sultan Murat II Mosque – built in 1450 for the Ottoman Sultan of the same name, though it was largely reconstructed in 2008 – and the Ganić Kula (fortified tower house) – which houses the local Heritage Museum – are two must-visits here.

9. Dobrilovina Monastery
⚑ L4

Near the town of Mojkovac, this 16th-century Serbian Orthodox monastery is a late and lesser-known example of the so-called Raška architectural style, which developed under medieval Serbia's powerful Nejmanić dynasty.

10. Berane
⚑ N3

Little-visited Berane is located on the River Lim – the banks of which are a popular swimming spot in summer. The nearby Đurđevi Stupovi Monastery, built in the 13th century, is one of its more famous landmarks. Berane is also home to a striking World War II memorial (Jasikovac Hill Monument), which is dedicated to the thousands killed here when Italian dictator Benito Mussolini put down the local Communist uprising.

The conical Jasikovac Hill Monument in Berane

Outdoor Activities

Epic scenery along the Durmitor Ring circuit

1. Cycling the Durmitor Ring
W summit.co.me
For an epic tour of the Durmitor massif on two wheels, nothing beats this 80-km (50-mile) circuit. The route starts in Žabljak and winds through the stunning scenery of the Tara and Sušica canyons. A guide is advised (*summit.co.me*).

2. Rafting on the Piva and Tara
Montenegro has some great rafting experiences at various points along both the Tara and Piva rivers, but the top accolade tends to go to the area around Šćepan Polje. Tours are easy to arrange (*montenegroadventure.travel*).

3. Hiking in Durmitor
There are plenty of short strolls in Durmitor, but the best views need to be earned. Multiday treks take travellers to the park's wildest viewpoints – try the hike to Lokvice, from where you can climb Bobotov Kuk (some scrambling experience and a good head for heights required) and Međed.

4. Canyoning in Nevidio
Jump and slide your way through this narrow canyon (not far from Durmitor) with Montenegro Canyoning (*montenegro-canyoning.com*) or Durmitor Adventure (*durmitoradventure.com*).

5. Cycling the Čakor Pass
The Čakor Pass, which tops out at 1,841 m (6,040 ft) on the road between Plav and the Rogova Gorge in Kosovo, has gained near-mythical status as a true back-of-beyond cycle route. The road, and pass, are closed to vehicles but open to cyclists, offering a steep but spectacular climb. Bear in mind that you'll need to get a permit from the border police station in Plav, and note that this is a politically sensitive and disputed border area.

6. Skiing in Savin Kuk
Durmitor's peaks may be better known for their hiking opportunities, but skiing is also popular here. Savin Kuk is the main ski resort, offering blue, red and black runs.

7. Zip-lining over the Tara River
Bungee jumping from the Đurđevića Tara Bridge may be a thing of the past (it closed down due to traffic issues) but the Tara Zip Line is a worthy replacement. Prepare to reach speeds of up to 120 km/h (75 mph) as you're launched across the canyon.

8. Horse Riding in the Highlands
Roam the wilds of Montenegro on horseback with Mountain Riders (*mountainriders.me*); note that some tours are restricted to experienced riders only.

9. Ride the Piva Zip Line
Race above the astonishing blue of Lake Piva on a 1,400-m (4,595-ft) zip line (the longest in Montenegro), with stunning views (*069 635 412*).

10. Paragliding above Durmitor
Along with the Bay of Kotor, Durmitor is one of the best spots in the country for paragliding. Paragliding Montenegro (*paragliding.me*) offers tandem flights over the stunning landscapes of the national park.

Places to Eat

1. Durmitorsko Sijelo
◹ K3 ◹ Savin Kuk bb, Žabljak
☎ 067 033 145 · €€

This little mountain hut at the foot of the Savin Kuk chairlift is a lovely place to refuel after a day on the slopes. It mostly serves classic Balkan cuisine.

2. Walter
◹ K3 ◹ Lučevača bb, Žabljak
🌐 walterbbq.me · €

Part of a chain with branches all over Serbia and Montenegro, this is the place in town to indulge in a plate of succulent, grilled *ćevapi* (finger-shaped meatballs). Plant-based versions of the dish are also available.

3. Restaurant Sočica
◹ J3 ◹ Plužine 🌐 parkpiva.com/en/listing/restoran-socica · €€

With a scenic location, rustic interior and great traditional food, this spot beside Lake Piva is a local go-to.

4. Restoran Jezero
◹ J3 ◹ Plužine 🌐 parkpiva.com/listing/restoran-jezero · €€

Bag a seat on the terrace of this popular restaurant for sweeping views of Lake Piva.

5. Restoran Most
◹ M4 ◹ Polja, Mojkovac ☎ 069 812 822 · €€

Feast on large portions of authentic Montenegrin dishes such as *kačamak* (p72) and *cicvara* (cornflour and cottage cheese porridge) at this friendly restaurant.

6. Restoran Kero
◹ Q3 ◹ Jaha Kurtagića, Rožaje
☎ 069 373 033 · €€

Hunker down in this cosy spot for tasty Balkan food, finished off with a *Turska kafa* (Turkish coffee).

7. Restoran Dobre Vode
◹ M5 ◹ E65, Sjenogoste ☎ 069 233 000 · €€

Perched on the road from Kolašin to Mojkovac, this local spot specializes in roasted and grilled meat.

8. Izvor
◹ K3 ◹ Jezerska Površ, Žabljak
☎ 067 661 300 · €€

Dine with epic views of the mountains at this low-key restaurant, in a rural setting on the road to Šavnik.

9. Café Missk
◹ P5 ◹ Racina bb, Plav ☎ 051 250 512 · €

Located right next to the bus station, this local favourite offers grilled dishes, soups, salads and pizzas.

10. Oro
◹ K3 ◹ Njegoševa 23, Žabljak
🌐 restaurantoro.me · €€

This is one of the best places to eat in Žabljak. Expect traditional dishes like lamb cutlets, grilled trout, *kačamak* and stuffed peppers.

**Diners on the terrace at Oro,
a popular choice in Žabljak**

STREETSMART

Crossing the Đurđevića Tara Bridge

GETTING AROUND

Whether you're visiting Montenegro for a short break or a week-long road trip, discover how best to reach your destination and travel around the country like a pro.

AT A GLANCE

PUBLIC TRANSPORT COSTS

PODGORICA

€1.00

(Single bus journey)

BUDVA TO KOTOR

€3.00

(Single bus journey)

PODGORICA TO BAR

€3.60

(Single rail journey)

SPEED LIMIT

BUILT-UP AREAS

50 km/h (32 mph)

OPEN ROAD

80 km/h (50 mph)

EXPRESSWAYS

100 km/h (62 mph)

Arriving by Air

Most flights from Europe land at Podgorica Airport in Golubovci, 11 km (7 miles) south of the capital, and Tivat Airport on the coast. The national carrier, **Air Montenegro**, offers flights to a dozen or so European cities, but currently none to the UK. Podgorica Airport offers year-round flights to the UK with **Ryanair**, while Tivat Airport offers seasonal flights (April to September) to the UK with **easyJet** and **Wizzair**. Many people choose to fly into Dubrovnik's Čilipi Airport, just 29 km (18 miles) across the Croatian border, which offers more flights to the UK and the rest of Europe. Flying from the USA will involve a change at a European hub.

Air Montenegro
w air-montenegro.com
easyJet
w easyjet.com
Ryanair
w ryanair.com
Wizzair
w wizzair.com

Trains

There are just two train lines in Montenegro, both run by **Railway Transport Montenegro**. The principal line runs from Bijelo Polje, near the Serbian border, to Bar via Podgorica. It's one of the world's most beautiful railway journeys, cutting through the mountains via a series of viaducts; the train continues to Belgrade, Serbia twice a day. A second line runs between Podgorica and Nikšić, northwest of the capital. Fares are calculated by distance travelled and are very cheap; the only train you need to reserve a seat on is the service from Belgrade to Bar.

Railway Transport Montenegro
w zpcg.me/en

Buses

In the absence of a comprehensive train network, Montenegro's bus links provide the best transport around the country. The network consists of an array of private companies and services are frequent, reliable and cheap.

Podgorica is the country's main transport hub, with buses fanning out from here to all parts of the country – though note that the interior is not nearly as well served as the coast. In Podgorica, tickets can be purchased at the counter or a self-service machine; alternatively, you can purchase tickets online at **BusTicket**, which also has full timetables. In smaller towns and villages, pay the driver.

BusTicket
W busticket4.me

Driving

The most common way to travel in Montenegro is by car. The main roads are generally in good condition, though minor roads are invariably poor, with many disintegrating and potholed, particularly in the mountain regions. Here, too, secondary roads can be completely closed by snow in winter. Winter tyres are required should the weather conditions deem them necessary. The main coastal road is in good condition, but suffers under the volume of traffic in the summer.

You must be aged 21 and have a valid driving licence to hire a car here. There are an increasing number of electric vehicle charging stations throughout the country, albeit most of these are currently located along the coast. A full list of charging points can be found on the **Electromaps** website.

Electromaps
W electromaps.com

Rules of the Road

In Montenegro drive on the right and overtake on the left. Headlights must be on and seat belts must be worn at all times, and it is forbidden to use a hand-held mobile phone while driving. The maximum blood alcohol limit is 0.03 per cent. The police *(policija)* are ubiquitous and it's not unusual to be pulled over randomly – make sure you

have all your documents with you, whether that's those of your own car or those of a hire car. For roadside assistance, contact **Auto-Moto Association Montenegro**.

Auto-Moto Association Montenegro
W fia.com

Taxis

Taxis are quite cheap and are generally metered in the larger towns; expect to pay around €0.50 per km within a city. All are available around the clock, but it's best to book ahead. In the capital, **City Taxi** and **Red Taxi** are go-tos.

City Taxi
C 19711

Red Taxi
C 19714

Cycling

Cycling is a fantastic and inexpensive way of seeing the country in summer. While many routes now have excellent signposting, inland roads can be in poor condition. You will need to be competent at repairing your bike, especially if cycling through the interior where facilities are sparse (make sure you have spares of everything). Your best bet for bike hire are agencies such as **Black Mountain Holidays** in Herceg Novi and **Bajković Bike** in Kotor, both of whom do bike tours.

Bajković Bike
W bajkovicbike.com

Black Mountain Holidays
W montenegroholiday.com

Walking

Montenegro's compact towns and cities are easy to explore on foot, with key sites within walking distance of each other. If you're planning to hike in the mountains, come equipped for variable weather and difficult terrain. The **Mountaineering Association of Montenegro** has a list of huts for long-distance hikes and can offer advice.

Mountaineering Association of Montenegro
W pscg.me

PRACTICAL INFORMATION

A little local know-how goes a long way in Montenegro. On these pages you can find all the essential advice and information you will need to make the most of your trip to this country.

AT A GLANCE

CURRENCY
Euro

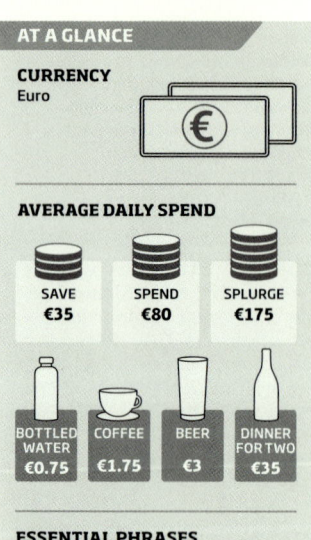

AVERAGE DAILY SPEND

SAVE	SPEND	SPLURGE
€35	€80	€175

BOTTLED WATER	COFFEE	BEER	DINNER FOR TWO
€0.75	€1.75	€3	€35

ESSENTIAL PHRASES

Hello	Zdravo
Goodbye	Do Viđenja
Please	Molim
Thank you	Hvala
Do you speak English?	Govorite li engleski?
I don't understand...	Ne razumijem

ELECTRICITY SUPPLY

Power sockets are type F, fitting two-pronged plugs. Standard voltage is 230v, 50Hz.

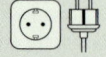

Passports and Visas

For entry requirements, including visas, consult your nearest Montenegrin embassy. Citizens of the UK, Australia, Canada, New Zealand and the US can visit Montenegro without a visa for up to 90 days in any 180-day period. Note that Montenegro is currently not part of the European Travel Information and Authorisation System (ETIAS).

Government Advice

It is always important to consult both your and the Montenegrin government's advice before travelling. The UK Foreign, Commonwealth and Development Office (**FCDO**), the **US Department of State**, the **Australian Department of Foreign Affairs and Trade** and the **Government of Montenegro** offer the latest information on security, health and local regulations.
Australian Department of Foreign Affairs and Trade
W smarttraveller.gov.au
FCDO
W gov.uk/foreign-travel-advice
Government of Montenegro
W gov.me
US Department of State
W state.gov/travel

Customs Information

There are strict rules about goods you can take into and out of Montenegro. Always declare items of value like expensive jewellery, and photographic and computer equipment. Upon entry and exit, you must declare cash or travellers' cheques if the value is €10,000 or more.

Insurance

We recommend that you take out a comprehensive insurance policy covering theft, loss of belongings, medical care, cancellations and delays. Remember to read the small print carefully, especially if you are planning to do any extreme sports such as whitewater rafting. UK citizens are eligible for free emergency medical care in Montenegro provided they have a European Health Insurance Card (EHIC) or UK Global Health Insurance Card (**GHIC**). US travellers should take out private health insurance.

GHIC

🔲 nhs.uk

Vaccinations

No vaccinations are required for Montenegro, although you may consider having hepatitis A, polio and typhoid boosters if you're planning to stay in more remote areas.

Money

Although Montenegro is not part of the European Union, it uses the euro as its defacto domestic currency. You'll find ATMs in all banks and most larger stores, malls and petrol stations. Credit and debit cards (including American Express) are now accepted by most hotels, shops, restaurants and petrol stations. Contactless payments are widely accepted across Montenegro. Although tipping is not obligatory, it is polite to offer between 5 and 10 per cent in restaurants and taxis.

Travellers with Specific Requirements

Historically, little attention has been paid to those with specific requirements in Montenegro, and while attitudes are slowly changing, those with limited mobility will find it quite tough going. Public transport is often poorly accessible, and cars with hand controls are rarely available from car-hire companies. Moreover, few museums or sights have much by way of disabled access, and many of the country's main sights – such as Kotor's Old Town and Stari Bar – are not conducive to getting around by wheelchair; it's always best to call ahead if you wish to visit a particular place. However, many

of the higher-end hotels along the coast have good access, with dedicated wheelchair-accessible rooms, and some beaches also cater to those with reduced mobility. The **Montenegro Health and Tourism Service** in Podgorica specializes in providing services to those with limited mobility.

It's advised that you carry a prescription for any drugs you need, including the generic name in case of emergency, and spares of any special clothing or equipment, as it's unlikely you'll find replacements in Montenegro.

Montenegro Health and Tourism Service

🔲 pantou.org/montenegro-health-and-tourism-service

Language

For years, Serbo-Croat was the language of Montenegro, Serbia, Bosnia and Croatia. Montenegro now calls its language Montenegrin, but to all intents and purposes, however, it is almost identical to Serbian, albeit with a few subtle differences, one being that Montenegrin has two extra letters in the alphabet. English proficiency is high among locals, particularly along the coast, although any attempt to speak Montenegrin will be appreciated by locals.

Opening Hours

In the capital and along the coast, shops generally open 9am to 7 or 8pm Monday to Saturday and 9am to 1pm Sunday; elsewhere, hours tend to be shorter. Grocery stores tend to open from 7am to 10pm, but usually close on Sunday. Banks and post offices open roughly from 8am to 7pm, Monday to Friday.

> Situations can change quickly and unexpectedly. Always check before visiting attractions and hospitality venues for up-to-date opening hours and booking requirements.

Personal Security

Montenegro is a generally safe country, with a low crime rate, but travellers should take the usual safety precautions: always lock your car, don't leave valuables on display and don't flash your cash. There are instances of petty theft, typically in crowded areas and on beaches. If you have anything stolen, report the crime within 24 hours to the nearest police station and take ID with you. Get a copy of the crime report to make an insurance claim.

In line with much of the Balkans, Montenegro is a socially conservative society, and tolerance towards the LGBTQ+ community can be low – discretion is therefore advised. However, times are changing: in 2020 the Montenegrin parliament voted to legalize same-sex civil partnerships, and Podgorica now hosts an annual LGBTQ+ pride march. **Queer Montenegro** offers advice for LGBTQ+ travellers visiting the country.

When hiking in Montenegro, note that not all trails are well marked, so a good stock of maps is recommended. Unlikely as it is that you'll encounter brown bears in the mountains (there are estimated to be only around 120), you might feel more comfortable carrying a whistle and/or bear spray.

Queer Montenegro
ⓦ queermontenegro.org

Health

Montenegro has a lower standard of healthcare than much of western Europe, but services are adequate. Emergency medical care is free for UK citizens in possession of a valid GHIC (*p125*). You may have to pay after treatment and reclaim the money when back home. In any case, it's essential that you arrange comprehensive medical insurance before you travel.

Montenegro's main hospitals include the **Clinical Centre of Montenegro**, in Podgorica, and the **General Hospital Kotor**. Pharmacies (*apoteka*) can be found in almost every town.

Avoid any contact with stray dogs, as there's a very slight risk of rabies. Travellers should also be aware of tick-borne encephalitis, which is contracted from the bite of a tick; these are prevalent between early spring to late autumn in forests and long grass. To avoid being bitten, apply tick repellent

---

AT A GLANCE

EMERGENCY NUMBERS

GENERAL EMERGENCY	POLICE
112	**122**

FIRE BRIGADE	AMBULANCE
123	**124**

TIME ZONE
Montenegro is one hour ahead of Greenwich Mean Time (GMT), and is six hours ahead of Eastern Standard Time (EST). Daylight saving time is observed here.

TAP WATER
Tap water is safe to drink throughout the country.

WEBSITES AND APPS

National Tourism Organization Montenegro
Montenegro's official tourism website (*montenegro.travel*).

Visit Montenegro
Website showing places of interest in Montenegro (*visit-montenegro.com*).

Black Mountain Adventure Travel
Popular tour operator organizing hiking trips (*montenegroholiday.com*).

and wear appropriate clothing: long trousers tucked into socks and boots, a hat and a long-sleeved top.

Clinical Centre of Montenegro
☎ 20 412 412
General Hospital Kotor
☎ 20 325 602

Smoking, Drugs and Alcohol

Smoking is banned in restaurants, cafés, bars and clubs. It is also forbidden to smoke on public transport.

The maximum blood alcohol limit for drivers is 0.03 per cent, although it is recommended that you should not consume anything if you plan to drive. Those caught over the limit will be fined, may temporarily or permanently lose their licence, and may be jailed.

Penalties for possession, use and trafficking of drugs are severe.

ID

You must always carry a form of ID, such as a photocard driving licence or passport, when in Montenegro. If you do not, the police can fine you.

Local Customs

When visiting churches and monasteries, modest clothing should be worn (some monasteries do provide covering). Shoes should be removed when visiting any of the country's mosques.

Responsible Travel

There are simple ways visitors can help towards Montenegro's sustainable tourism goals. Embrace locally and sustainably sourced cuisine, carry a refillable water bottle (there are plenty of places to fill up) and use public transport wherever possible. If you're considering booking a tour or outdoor activity, **Undiscovered Montenegro** is a great choice. The company donates a proportion of its profits to the local Dalmatian Pelican Conservation Project and organizes regular clean-ups of Lake Skadar.

Be mindful that cruise ship tourism is extremely popular around the Bay of Kotor. Travellers should plan their visit accordingly – CruiseMapper is a useful app (p33) – to avoid overwhelming the small towns here. If you have booked a cruise, try to explore independently (supporting local businesses instead of booking a package with the cruise liner) when you disembark.

Undiscovered Montenegro
🅆 undiscoveredmontenegro.com

Mobile Phones and Wi-Fi

As Montenegro is not in the EU, roaming charges apply for all travellers here. As a result, it is worth investing in a Montenegrin SIM card (typically costing around €5), which you can top up with vouchers from mobile providers, post offices and kiosks. Coverage is generally excellent, but can be patchy in the mountainous inland areas. Wi-Fi is standard in all accommodation facilities as well as restaurants and cafés.

Postal Services

Post offices can be found in most towns and are open 8am to 8pm Monday to Friday, sometimes closing earlier in smaller towns. Stamps are sold at post offices as well as newsagents and kiosks. **Montenegro Post** runs the country's postal system.

Montenegro Post
🅆 postacg.me

Taxes and Refunds

Montenegro is part of the European Tax Free Shopping system, with VAT charged at 19 per cent. The minimum purchase amount for which tax can be refunded is €100, but note that not all stores provide this service, so ask before making a purchase.

Discount Cards

If you're planning to visit multiple national parks in Montenegro, it could be worth purchasing the annual national park pass from the **National Parks of Montenegro** website.

National Parks of Montenegro
🅆 nparkovi.me

PLACES TO STAY

Montenegro's accommodation is mostly focused along its coastline, where you'll find a wealth of high-end hotels that cater to the tourist crowd. While there are fewer options inland, Podgorica still offers a clutch of good hotels and Northern Montenegro promises a range of rural retreats.

Accommodation along the coast can fill up during the busy summer months, so it's always worth booking in advance. While visiting off-season is generally cheaper, many coastal amenities close in the winter.

PRICE CATEGORIES

For a standard, double room per night (with breakfast if included), taxes and extra charges.

€ under €100
€€ €100–250
€€€ over €250

Bay of Kotor

Hotel Conte
B2 Obala Marko Martinovića, Perast hotelconte.me · €€

Few hotels have a more scenic location than this former palace. Comprising a collection of white stone buildings, Hotel Conte is perfectly perched on the edge of the Bay of Kotor. You'll want to bag a room with a view of the water, but don't worry if you can't. Instead, soak up the scenery from the hotel's restaurant: its edge-of-the-water location pairs perfectly with the seafood menu.

Garni Hotel Bokeska Noc
A3 Braće Grahalića 42, Herceg Novi 31 345 788 · €

A rare find along Montenegro's resort-centric coastline, this family-run hotel promises modestly sized, but comfortable, double and triple rooms – many of which have elevated views of the sparkling Adriatic. The real highlight, however, is breakfast on the flower-filled garden terrace; it's a wonderful spread, prepared by the friendly owner himself, and features a different home-cooked local dish every day.

Lazure Hotel
A3 Braće Pedišića bb, Meljine lazurehotel.com · €€€

This is one of the bay's most beautiful hotels. Rooms – with designer furniture sourced from Serbia and Italy – have either sea, garden or courtyard views, while the dazzling lobby is centred on a stylish wine bar. As for amenities, there's an indoor pool, hamman, sauna and jacuzzi, plus a private pebble beach. What more could you ask for?

Hotel Forza Mare
B3 Kriva ul Dobrota, Dobrota forzahotels.com · €€€

The rooms in this glamorous retreat are top-notch, but what you're really here for is the sweeping view of the Bay of Kotor. And the hotel's outdoor area is the best place to enjoy it. Picture a diminutive pebble beach fringed by palms and dotted with rattan sun beds, with an outdoor whirlpool tub and a small turquoise mosaic-tiled pool nearby. Steps leading down into the shimmering bay waters are the cherry on top.

Hotel Palazzo Radomiri
B3 Dobrota 220, Dobrota palazzo radomiri.com · €€€

This former aristocratic mansion of a shipping family is now a graceful boutique hotel. It hosts ten stunning rooms, each featuring exposed walls, Baroque wooden furniture and marble bathrooms. Facilities are just as noteworthy, with an outdoor pool and spa, mini-gym and a delightful walled garden restaurant. The complimentary morning yoga classes, hosted by the owner, Anna, are another bonus.

Hotel Hippocampus

B3 **Stari Grad 489, Kotor** **hotelhippocampus.com · €€**

Occupying a renovated 17th-century Venetian palazzo, Hippocampus (meaning "seahorse") is Kotor's swankiest outfit. While its nine rooms lack dramatic views, owing to the building's tight configuration, this is more than compensated for with its fixtures and fittings: Nepalese stone floors, wooden ceilings, bespoke velvet sofas and abstract artwork splashed across the walls. Its greatest triumph, however, is the rooftop terrace bar, perfect for a sundowner.

Eco Hotel Carrubba

B3 **Donja Lastva bb, Donja Lastva** **septembrehotels.com · €€**

Named after the handsome carob tree outside, this lovely little hotel scores highly for its eco-credentials. For starters, it features solar panels, geothermal heating and a wastewater treatment system. On top of that, its restaurant menu is dominated by organic ingredients, so you can feast and feel good doing it.

Hotel Chedi

B3 **Luštica Bay, Radovići** **lusticabay.com · €€€**

Luxury is the name of the game at this spectacular five-star hotel. It's set over four levels, starting with a soaring glass lobby (where guests receive a complimentary glass of bubbly upon arrival) and extending to a series of slick, sunlit rooms (where oak joinery meets limestone flooring and mirrored walls). Outside, the gorgeous infinity pool is a lovely place to cool down.

Regent

B3 **Porto Montenegro, Tivat** **regenthotels.com · €€€**

Overlooking Porto Montenegro's superyacht marina, this grand hotel comprises two buildings: the Venezia wing, inspired by noble Venetian-Renaissance architecture, and the more contemporary Aqua wing. But it's the pools that are the highlight. There are three here: an indoor seaview pool with a hot tub, an outdoor pool on the first-floor terrace and, between the two hotel wings, a vast infinity pool ringed by sunbeds and tropical palms.

Old Town Hostel

B3 **Stari Grad 284, Kotor** **hostel-kotor.me · €**

Ensconced within a fabulous palazzo, this welcoming hostel sometimes feels more like a boutique hotel. Comprising two wings, Old Town Hostel features communal living rooms and a host of en-suite dorms. Staff are always on hand to help (when they're not leading a guided walking tour of Kotor or organizing barbecue nights and boat parties, that is).

The Coast

Hotel Budva

C4 **Slovenska obala bb, Budva** **hotel-budva.net · €€**

From the grand porticoed entrance to the marble stairs in the lobby, it's clear that this Neo-Classically styled hotel – just a pebble's throw from the beach – is something special. Rooms are very much on the snazzy side, but the hotel's real calling card is its second-floor infinity pool and bar.

Dukley Hotel and Resort

C4 **Jadranska put, Zavala Peninsula Budva** **dukleyhotels.com · €€€**

Perched right on the water, this five-star family resort ticks all the boxes. There's a wide selection of accommodation, from standard rooms to four-bed suites; a wealth of dining options, including beach bars and Montenegro's first kosher restaurant; and a fabulous infinity pool. With so much on offer, you won't want to leave the complex.

Hotel Vissi d'Arte

C4 **Mediteranska 10, Budva** **hotelvissidarte. com · €€€**

The art of hospitality is on full display at this modern hotel. Welcoming staff always go above and beyond to help guests, whether they're assisting with restaurant bookings or providing local recommendations. The hotel is equally impressive: a shiny glass structure between the marina and the Old Town (all rooms have private furnished balconies).

Villa Geba

C4 **Vukice Mitrovic, Sveti Stefan** **villageba. com · €€€**

Tucked into the folds of a hillside overlooking the picture-postcard islet of Sveti Stefan, this is luxury of a different level. There are seven suites, each one named for a different mythological figure and each with a sea-facing terrace. The fine-dining restaurant, Muse, is also something to write home about.

Montebay Villa

C4 **Buljarica 2, Buljarica** **montebay villa.com · €€€**

Want to escape the hustle and bustle of the coast? Hunker down at Montebay. This stone-built villa is hidden away in a secluded corner of Buljarica, close to wetlands teeming with birdlife. Some rooms may be basic, but the outdoor pool (with sweeping

views towards the coast) and the hotel's exquisite French cooking more than make up for it.

Eco Resort Cermeniza

D4 **Virpazar** **cermeniza.com · €€**

Locations don't get much better than this in Montenegro – and that's saying something. Nine sumptuously furnished stone villas are nestled near Lake Skadar, amid a lush landscape of rolling hills and vineyards (one owned by the hotel). At the heart of the complex there's also a lovely outdoor pool (if you don't fancy a lake swim).

Stara Carsija Hotel

D5 **Starobarska čaršija 243, Stari Bar** **staracarsija.me · €€€**

Abutting the ruins of Stari Bar, this rustically styled hotel is very much in keeping with its surrounds (think lots of exposed white stone, chunky wooden bedsteads and handwoven rugs). An outdoor pool, Finnish sauna and hammam round things off in style.

Hotel Barjaktar

E6 **Vida Matanovica 5/2, Ulcinj** **barjaktar.me · €€€**

Treat yourself at this quality boutique hotel. It sports a selection of bright, light-filled rooms, suites and apartments, most promising shimmering sea views. More views await from the

roof terrace, which hosts a mini pool and jacuzzi. Still need more to tempt you? Consider the hotel's on-site winery and private boat tours.

Palata Venezia

E6 **Stari Grad, Ulcinj** **hotelpalatavenezia. com · €€€**

Enviably sited on a bluff overlooking Ulcinj's harbour, this trim whitestone building has a mix of high-class rooms and apartments, all with polished dark wood furnishings and splendid views. There's a classy restaurant and wine bar, too.

Central Montenegro

Hotel Hemera

E3 **Njegoševa 17, Podgorica** **hotel hemera.com · €€**

Urban chic meets quirky industrial in this smart city-centre hotel, with polished concrete walls, sofas upholstered in red velvet and Persian rugs. While there's a wellness centre, complete with sauna and Turkish bath, the main attraction is Hotel Hemera's buzzy city location. Step outside and you're in the thick of Podgorica's boisterous café district.

Hilton Podgorica Crna Gora

E3 **Bul Sv Petra Cetinjshog 2, Podgorica** **hilton.com · €€**

A tip-top renovation has turned this into the city's

premier hotel, and while it is ostensibly aimed at business travellers, it's personable enough to make it an attractive proposition to all – not least the city's only rooftop bar, open to both guests and visitors.

Hotel Sokoline
? D2 **⌂** Poštanski fah 35, Danilovgrad **W** hotel-sokoline.me · €€

Built on a cliff with an unbeatable mountain panorama from its open terrace, the "falcon" hotel has a good mix of standard rooms sleeping two and apartments sleeping four, each with its own private balcony to enjoy the scenery.

Northern and Eastern Montenegro

Four Points Sheraton
? M5 **⌂** Radoša Mašhovicća bb, Kolašin **W** fourpointsholasin.com · €€

This classy alpine-style hotel offers all the requisite comforts after a busy day on the slopes (think cosy, wood-clad rooms, big fluffy duvets and thick carpets). Factor in a fourth-floor buffet restaurant, ground-floor café, small spa and gym, and you've got one impressive ensemble. Ski-hire facilities and free shuttle bus services to local ski resorts make this a particularly attractive option during the winter.

Hotel Žabljak
? K3 **⌂** Trg Durmitorshih, Žabljah **W** hmdurmitor.com · €€

There's a range of accommodation in the mountain town of Žabljak, but this one is a favourite. A triangular-shaped building presiding over the main square, it promises good-sized rooms with big beds, a small playroom for the kids and an accomplished restaurant. As for the surrounds, this is hiking territory at its very best.

Hotel SOA
? K3 **⌂** Put za Crno Jezero **W** hotelsoa.com · €€

Want a space away from the buzz of Žabljak? Check in to this quieter hotel, on the road to the Black Lake. You're right on the edge of Durmitor National Park here, with spectacular hikes just a hop, skip and a jump away. Inside, the hotel's lovely: the wine bar is a super spot to kick back and staff are friendly and attentive.

Etno Selo Montenegro
? J4 **⌂** Brezna, Piva **W** etnoselo.me · €

Situated amid lovely wildflower meadows, this is Montenegro's original – and still best – ethno village. There are 25 authentically furnished wood and stone cottages plus a rustic taverna, where guests can enjoy roast lamb, among other dishes. Beneath the restaurant

there's a small museum displaying various knick-knacks; this is also where the owners stash their store of homemade red wine, which guests are welcome to sample.

Etno Selo Izlazak
? J3 **⌂** Rudinice, Plužine **W** etno-selo-izlazah.me · €

If tucking into hearty mountain food on an open-air terrace overlooking the Piva Canyon sounds like your kind of afternoon, book a room at this hotel. Stunningly sited high above the yawning canyon, it offers an impressive mix of accommodation, including wooden bungalows, larger cottages and stone-built apartments. Staff can also organize rafting trips along the nearby Tara River.

Camp Grab
? J2 **⌂** Brijeg, near Šćepan Polje **W** tara-grab.com · €

Outdoor types make a beeline for this local campsite. It's tucked away in the far corner of the country, on the border with Bosnia and Herzegovina, and offers outdoor activities galore. Guests can go rafting, biking, hiking or canyoning, all organized by the experienced team here. Accommodation-wise, there's a mix of bungalows and camping grounds, as well as a waterside terrace-cum-bar where buffet-style meals are served.

Index

Page numbers in **bold** refer to main entries.

PHRASE BOOK

Pronunciation Guide

c	"ts" as in rats	č	"ch" as in church
ć	"t" is a soft t	đ	"d" as in endure
g	"g" as in get	j	"y" as in yes
š	"sh" as in shoe	ž	"J" as in Jacques

In an Emergency

Help!	Upomoć!	oopomoch!
Stop!	Stani!	stahnee!
Call a doctor!	Zovite ljekara!	zoveetey lyehkara!
Call an ambulance!	Zovite hitnu pomoć!	zoveetey heetnoo pomoch!
Call the police!	Zovite policiju!	zoveetey poleetseeyoo!
Call the fire brigade!	Zovite vatrogasce!	zoveetey vatrohgastsay!
Where is the nearest telephone?	Gdje je najbliži telefon?	gdyey yey nigh bleezhee telefon
Where is the nearest hospital?	Gdje je najbliža bolnica?	gdyey yey n-igh bleezhah bolnitsa

Communication Essentials

Yes	Da	dah
No	Ne	neh
Please	Molim vas	moleem vas
Thank you	Hvala	hvahlah
Excuse me	Oprostite	oprosteetey
Hello	Dobar dan	dobar dan
Goodbye	Doviđenja	doveedjenya
Good night	Laku noć	lakoo noch
Yesterday	Juče	yoocheh
Today	Danas	danas
Tomorrow	Sutra	sootrah
Month	mesec	mehsehts
Week	nedelja	nehdehlyah
Morning	jutro	yootroh
Afternoon	popodne	pohpodneh
Evening	veče	vehcheh
Night	noć	noch
Year	godina	gohdeenah
Here	Tu	too
There	Tamo	tahmoh
What?	Šta?	shtah
When?	Kada?	kada
Why?	Zašto?	zashtoh
Where?	Gdje?	gdyey

Useful Phrases

How are you?	Kako ste?	kakoh stey
Very well, thank you	Dobro, hvala	dobroh, hvahlah
Pleased to meet you	Drago mi je!	dragoh mee yeh
See you soon	Vidimo se	veedeemoh seh
That's fine	U redu	oo rehdoo
Where is/are...?	Gdje je/su...?	gdyey yey/soo
How far is it to...?	Koliko je daleko do...?	kohleekoh yey dalekoh doh

How can I get to...?	Kako mogu doći do...?	kakoh mogoo dohchee doh
Do you speak English?	Govorite li engleski?	govoreeteh lee engleskee
I don't understand	Ne razumijem	neh rahzoomeeyem
Could you speak more slowly please?	Molim vas, možete li da govorite sporije?	moleem vas, mozhetey lee dah govoreeteh spohreeyeh
I'm sorry	Žao mi je	zhaoh mee yeh

Useful Words

big	veliko	veleekoh
small	malo	mahloh
hot	vruće	vroocheh
cold	hladno	hlahdnoh
good	dobro	dohbroh
bad	loše	lohsheh
enough	dosta	dohstah
open	otvoreno	ohtvohrenoh
closed	zatvoreno	zatvohrenoh
left	lijevo	leeyehvoh
right	desno	dehsnoh
straight ahead	pravo napred	prahvoh nahpred
near	blizu	bleezoo
far	daleko	dahlehkoh
up	gore	gohreh
down	dolje	dohlyeh
early	rano	rahnoh
late	kasno	kahsnoh
entrance	ulaz	oolaz
exit	izlaz	eezlahz
toilet	WC	vehtseh
more	više	veesheh
less	manje	mahnyeh

Shopping

How much does this cost?	Koliko ovo košta?	kohleekoh ohvoh kohshta?
I would like...	Voleo bih...	vohlehoh beeh...
Do you have...?	Imate li...?	eematey lee...?
I'm just looking	Samo gledam	Sahmoh glehdam
Do you take credit cards?	Primate li kreditne kartice?	preemateh lee credeetneh carteetseh
What time do you open/close?	Kada otvarate/ zatvarate?	kahdah ohtvarateh/ zahtvarateh
This one	Ovaj	ohvigh
That one	Onaj	ohnigh
expensive	skupo	skoopoh
cheap	jeftino	yefteenoh
size (clothes)	veličina	vehleecheenah
size (shoes)	broj	broy
white	bijelo	beeyehloh
black	crno	tsrnoh
red	crveno	tsrvenoh
yellow	žuto	zhootoh
green	zeleno	zehlenoh
blue	plavo	plahvoh

bakery	pekara	*pehkarah*
bank	banka	*bahnkah*
book shop	knjižara	*knyeezharah*
butcher's	mesara	*mehsarah*
cake shop	poslastičarnica	*pohslastee charneetsah*
chemist's	apoteka	*apohtekah*
fishmonger's	ribarnica	*reebarnitsah*
market	tržnica	*trzhneetsah*
hairdresser's	frizer	*freezer*
newsagent's	kiosk	*keeosk*
post office	pošta	*pohshtah*

Sightseeing

entrance ticket	ulaznica	*oohlahzneetsah*
gallery	galerija	*gahlereeyah*
cathedral	katedrala	*kahtedralah*
church	crkva	*tsrkvah*
library	biblioteka	*beebleeohtehkah*
museum	muzeja	*moozehyah*
tourist information centre	turistički info punktovi	*tooreesteechkey eenfoh puhnktohvee*
bus station	autobuska stanica	*ahootohbooska stahnitsah*
railway station	željeznička stanica	*zhelehznichkah stahnitsah*
theatre	pozorište	*pohzohreeshteh*

Staying in a Hotel

Do you have a vacant room?	Imate li sobu?	*eematey lee sohboo*
double room	dvokrevetna soba	*dvokrevetnah sohbah*
single room	jednokrevetna soba	*yednokrevetnah sohbah*
room with a bathroom	soba sa kupatilom	*sohbah sah koopahteelohm*
shower	tuš	*toosh*
I have a reservation	Imam rezervaciju	*eemam rezervatseeyoo*

Eating Out

Have you got a table for…?	Imate li sto za…?	*eematey lee stoh zah*
I want to reserve a table	Želim da rezervišem sto	*Zheleem da rezerveeshem stoh*
The bill please	Molim vas, račun	*moleem vas, rachoon*
I am a vegetarian	Ja sam vegetarijanac	*yah sam vegetareeyanats*
waiter/waitress	konobar/ konobarica	*konobar/ konobaritsah*
menu	jelovnik	*yelovneek*
wine list	vinska karta	*veenskah kartah*
glass	čaša	*chashah*
bottle	flaša	*flahshah*
knife	nož	*nozh*
fork	viljuška	*veelyuhshka*
spoon	kašika	*kahsheekah*
breakfast	doručak	*doroochak*
lunch	ručak	*roochak*
dinner	večera	*vecherah*

main course	glavno jelo	*glavnoh yeloh*
starters	predjela	*predyelah*

Menu Decoder

bijela riba	*beeyelah reebah*	"white" fish
blitva	*bleetvah*	Swiss chard
riblja čorba	*reeblyah chorbah*	fish stew
ćevapčići	*chevapcheechee*	meatballs
crni rižoto	*tsrnee reezhotoh*	black risotto
desert	*desert*	dessert
glavno jelo	*glavnoh yeloh*	main course
pasulj	*pahsuly*	beans
gulaš	*goolash*	goulash
jastoga	*yastogah*	lobster
supa	*soohpah*	soup
kuvano	*koovahnoh*	cooked
maslinovo ulje	*masleenovoh oolyey*	olive oil
meso na žaru	*mesoh nah zharoo*	barbecued meat
miješano meso	*meejeshanoh mesoh*	mixed grilled meats
na žaru	*nah zharoo*	barbecued
sirće	*seercheh*	vinegar
palačinke	*palacheenkay*	pancakes
paprika	*papreekah*	pepper
pečeno	*pechenoh*	baked
piletina	*peeleteenah*	chicken
predjelo	*predyeloh*	starters
prilog	*preelog*	side dish
pršut	*prshoot*	smoked ham
pržene lignje	*przhene leegnyey*	fried squid
prženo	*przhenoh*	fried
ramsteak	*ramsteyk*	rump steak
ražnjići	*razhnyeechee*	pork kebabs
riba na žaru	*reebah nah zharoo*	barbecued fish
rižot frutti di mare	*reezhot frootee dee marey*	seafood risotto
rižot sa škampima	*reezhot sah shkampeemah*	scampi risotto
salata	*salatah*	salad
salata od hobotnice	*salatah od hobotneetsey*	octopus salad
sarma	*sarmah*	stuffed cabbage leaves
sir	*seer*	cheese
sladoled	*sladoled*	ice cream
slane sardine	*slaneh sardeeneh*	salted sardines
škampi	*shkampee*	scampi
školjke	*shkolkay*	shellfish
špageti frutti di mare	*shpagetee frootee dee marey*	spaghetti with seafood
sol	*sol*	salt
tjestenina	*tjesteneenah*	pasta
ulje	*oolyey*	oil

Drinks

bijelo vino	*beeyeloh veenoh*	white wine
crno vino	*tsrnoh veenoh*	red wine
gazirana/ negazirana mineralna voda	*gazeeranah/ neygazeeranah meeneralnah vodah*	sparkling/still mineral water
čaj	*ch-igh*	tea
kafa	*kafah*	coffee
pivo	*peevoh*	beer

Numbers

0	nula	*noolah*
1	jedan	*yedan*

2	**dva**	*dvah*	500	**petsto**	***pet**stoh*
3	**tri**	*tree*	700	**sedamsto**	*sedamstoh*
4	**četiri**	*cheteeree*	900	**devetsto**	*devetstoh*
5	**pet**	*pet*	1,000	**tisuću**	*teesoochoo*
6	**šest**	*shest*			
7	**sedam**	*sedam*	**Time**		
8	**osam**	*osam*	one minute	**jedna**	*yednah*
9	**devet**	*devet*		**minuta**	*meenootah*
10	**deset**	*deset*	one hour	**jedan sat**	*yedan saht*
11	**jedanaest**	*yedanighst*	half an hour	**pola sata**	*polah sahtah*
12	**dvanaest**	*dvahnighst*	Monday	**ponedjeljak**	*ponedyelyak*
13	**trinaest**	*treenighst*	Tuesday	**utorak**	*ootorak*
14	**četrnaest**	*chetrnighst*	Wednesday	**srijeda**	*sreejedah*
15	**petnaest**	*petnight*	Thursday	**četvrtak**	*chetvrtak*
16	**šesnaest**	*shestnighst*	Friday	**petak**	*petak*
17	**sedamnaest**	*sedamnighst*	Saturday	**subota**	*soobotah*
18	**osamnaest**	*osamnighst*	Sunday	**nedjelja**	*nedyelyah*
19	**devetnaest**	*devetnighst*	January	**januar**	*yahnooahr*
20	**dvadeset**	*dvahdeset*	February	**februar**	*febrooahr*
21	**dvadeset i**	*dvahdeset ee*	March	**mart**	*mart*
	jedan	*yedan*	April	**april**	*ahpreel*
30	**trideset**	*treedeset*	May	**maj**	*migh*
31	**trideset i**	*treedeset ee*	June	**jun**	*yoon*
	jedan	*yedan*	July	**jula**	*yoolah*
40	**četrdeset**	*chetrdeset*	August	**avgust**	*ahvgoost*
50	**pedeset**	*pedeset*	September	**septembar**	*sehptehmbar*
60	**šezdeset**	*shezdeset*	October	**oktobar**	*ohktohbar*
70	**sedamdeset**	*sedamdeset*	November	**novembar**	*nohvehmbar*
80	**osamdeset**	*osamdeset*	December	**decembar**	*dehtsembar*
90	**devedeset**	*devedeset*	spring	**proleće**	*prolehcheh*
100	**sto**	*stoh*	summer	**leto**	*lehtoh*
101	**sto i jedan**	*stoh ee yedan*	autumn (fall)	**jesen**	*yehsehn*
102	**sto i dva**	*stoh ee dvah*	winter	**zima**	*zeemah*
200	**dvjesto**	*dvyestoh*			

ACKNOWLEDGMENTS

Contributors Rudolf Abraham, Nicola Gibbs, Norm Longley, Justin McDonnell

Project Editor Lucy Sara-Kelly

Senior Editor Alison McGill

Senior Designers Laura O'Brien, Vinita Venugopal

Editors Charlie Baker, Rachel Laidler, Molly McCarthy, Tijana Todorinović

Proofreader Kathryn Glendenning

Indexer Helen Peters

Picture Researcher Naomi McMullen

Publishing Assistant Simona Velikova

Jacket Designer Laura O'Brien, Vinita Venugopal

Jacket Picture Researcher Pippa Seager

Senior Cartographic Editors Subhashree Bharati, James Macdonald

Cartography Manager Suresh Kumar

Senior DTP Designer Tanveer Zaidi

DTP Designer Rohit Rojal

Production Controller Kariss Ainsworth

Managing Art Editor Gemma Doyle

Senior Managing Art Editor Priyanka Thakur

Editorial Director Hollie Teague

Art Director Maxine Pedliham

Publishing Director Georgina Dee

The publisher would like to thank the following for their kind permission to reproduce their photographs:

Key: a-above; b-below/bottom; c-center; f-far; l-left; r-right; t-top

Alamy Stock Photo: Alpineguide 35tl; Antiqua Print Gallery 9tl; Jon Arnold Images Ltd 1; Child of the forest 21cla; Chronicle 35br; ClickAlps / mauritius images GmbH 34tl; Matjaz Corel 108bc; Svetlana Day 79bl; Pavel Dudek 55br; Tatiana Dyuvbanova 31tr; Efesenko 101bl; Greg Balfour Evans 91tr; Kirk Fisher 14bl; Elizaveta Galitckaia 25br; GARDEL Bertrand / hemis.fr 16cr; Hemis 47cra; Hemis 86br; Hemis 19; Hemis 62bc; 78tl; Imagebroker.com Gmbh & Co. Kg 53tl; Imagebroker.com Gmbh & Co. Kg 106tl; Mikhail Kokhanchikov 58tc; Ivan Kuznetsov 60br; Ranko Maras 87br; Mauritius Images Gmbh 96tl; Angus McComiskey 48bl; Hugh Mitton 107tc; Alexander Nikiforov 37bl; Alexander Nikiforov 49br;

Alexander Nikiforov 71bc; Ollirg 51; Irina Papoyan 57tl; Toma Paunovic 41tl; Matyas Rehak 46bc; Alexandre ROSA 47cla; Boaz Rottem / Stockimo 79tr; Shotshop GmbH 84bc; Egmont Strigl / imageBROKER.com GmbH & Co. KG 8; Olena Suvorova 60-61tc; vivoo 90bl; Darko Vrcan 111br; Jason Wells 88tc; Wirestock, Inc. 89bl; Jan Wlodarczyk 5.

AWL Images: J Banks 12cla; J Banks 22tc; J Banks 92–93tc; Hemis 83tc; Hemis 103tr; Hemis 110–111tc; Doug Pearson 15bl; Doug Pearson 74br.

Bridgeman Images: Archives Charmet / Bridgeman Images 9br; John Bethell 9cr.

Hotel & Restaurant Conte: 15.

Dreamstime.com: Sorin Colac 20crb; Dudlajzov 16bl; Fotokon 33br; Ioannaalexa 31br; Jana Janina 116bl; Jasmina 47tc; Mariana Karpova 114–115bc; Lucertolone 25tl; Aliaksandr Mazurkevich 114tl; Moreno Novello / Dreamstime.com 11br; Pfeifferv 12br; Photozlaja 72bl; Rndmst 116tr; Sergion777 100tc; Volodymyr Shevchuk 95bc; Travellingtobeprecise 106br; Lukas Vejrik 27bc; Lukas Vejrik 99tr; Igor Zivkovic 113tc.

Getty Images: AFP 10tl; ROBERT ATANASOVSKI / AFP 11tc; Ccr_358 29bc; DIMITAR DILKOFF / AFP 10bl; Imagebroker / Peter Schickert 63br; CHRISTOPHE SIMON / AFP 10cl; Paul Thompson / FPG / Archive Photos 10br; Jean-Philippe Tournut 85tl; Konstantin Voronov 32tc; Konstantin Voronov 96–97bc; Konstantin Voronov 104bc; Feng Wei Photography 44br; Feng Wei Photography 121; Westend61 27tl.

Getty Images / iStock: ioanna_alexa 30bc; AscentXmedia 6–7; Rob Atherton 42br; Avpod 37br; Belikart 23tr; Extreme-Photographer 69; Fotoember 37cb; Frantic00 98–99bc; Frantic00 57br; Givaga 45tc; Guruxoox 17bc; heckepics 13cr; Andrea Izzotti 66bl; Zoran Kolundzija 66tr; Bogdan Lazar 13tl; Letty17 23br; Lovcen 54tl; Stanislav_Moroz 15br; Nadtochiy 13bl; Naeblys 48–49tc; NataGolubnycha 95tr; Ns Propellers 68tc; Ivica Pavicic 86-87tc; A Periam Photography 21crb; A Periam Photography 29tl; Danijela Racic 73br; Rusm 20cl; Dmitrii Sakharov 15tr; Dmitrii Sakharov 16tr; SeppFriedhuber 24bl; Sevaljevic 28tc; skynesher 65bl; skynesher 74tl; Predrag Vuckovic 73tl; Wirestock 40–41bc; Zocha_K 67bc.

Top Hill Club: Milos Cetkovic 75tc.

JU KC "Nikola Djurkovic" Kotor: Krsto Vulovic 12cr; Krsto Vulovic 76–77bc.

Kotor Cable Car: 70tr.

Mary Evans Picture Library: Mirys Picture No.70. 9tr.

eji Kotor: 83br.

onal Museum of Montenegro: 52tl.

ional Tourism Organisation of ntenegro: Nebojsa Atanackovic 64tr.

toran Oro: 119br.

tterstock.com: Amyrxa 42tc; Novak Elcic a; Fotokon 13clb; Taras Hipp 13cl; kizaru43 Vadym Lavra 12clb; Mazur Travel 38–39tc; bl; Mileta V 117bc; Mo Wu 105tl; Jaroslav avcik 47tr; Lukas Vejrik 36tc; Stanislav nets 60bl.

nmit Tourist Agency Durmitor: 118tl.

ern Lanterna: 109tl.

ipa Cave Ltd: Igor Beni 59br.

istička organizacija Optine abljak: 24tr.

er Images:

t and Spine: **Alamy Stock Photo:** Wlodarczyk;
: **Dreamstime.com**: Volodymyr Shevchuk tr;
ty Images / iStock: Avpod cl, heckepics tl.

et Map Cover Image:

ny Stock Photo: Jan Wlodarczyk.

A NOTE FROM DK

The rate at which the world is changing is constantly keeping the DK travel team on our toes. While we've worked hard to ensure that this edition of Montenegro is accurate and up-to-date, we know that opening hours alter, standards shift, prices fluctuate, places close and new ones pop up in their stead. So, if you notice we've got something wrong or left something out, we want to hear about it. Please get in touch at travelguides@dk.com

Within each Top 10 list in this book, no hierarchy of quality or popularity is implied. All 10 are, in the editor's opinion, of roughly equal merit.

First edition 2025

Published in Great Britain by Dorling
Kindersley Limited, DK, 20 Vauxhall Bridge Road,
London SW1V 2SA

The authorised representative in the EEA is
Dorling Kindersley Verlag GmbH. Arnulfstr.
124, 80636 Munich, Germany

Published in the United States by DK Publishing,
1745 Broadway, 20th Floor, New York, NY 10019, USA

Copyright © 2025 Dorling Kindersley Limited
A Penguin Random House Company

25 26 27 28 29 10 9 8 7 6 5 4 3 2 1

A CIP catalog record for this book
is available from the British Library.

A catalog record for this book is available
from the Library of Congress.

ISSN: 1479-344X
ISBN: 978-0-2417-3321-9

Printed and bound in China

www.dk.com

This book was made with Forest
Stewardship Council™ certified
paper – one small step in DK's
commitment to a sustainable future.
Learn more at **www.dk.com/uk/
information/sustainability**